The
SECRET
to knowing it's
ALREADY
DONE!

Alex Morton

DEDICATION

This book is dedicated to the man who pushed me to pursue my dreams: My father, Marc Morton, who remains one of my greatest mentors, role models, and one of my best friends.

Dad, thank you for teaching me how to DREAM BIG, work hard, believe in myself, and never give up. You've taught me that success goes beyond any one area of life. You have held me to a high standard and taught me about integrity, humility, and character. Anybody who has been in the same room with you has felt the vibrancy of your Spirit. Your authenticity and your genuine care for others have kept you plugged in and enthusiastic about life. You've shown me the value of trials and setbacks, teaching me to always land on my feet. Thank you for reminding me about the joy and fullness of life found in every moment spent with the people who love and support us.

There have never been conditions on the love and support you have shown your children, and your selfless desire to support us in every season of life means the world to me. You inspire me to become more, especially in what matters most. Because of you, I'll be a great father, husband, brother, leader, and human being. Thanks for always being there and believing
in me.

I love you!

BOOMER SOONER,
Your Son, Alex

AUTHOR'S NOTE

These words are from the spoken words
of my late friend and mentor,
Bob Proctor,
as taken from an audio
that he sent me:

A MESSAGE FROM BOB PROCTOR

I want to tell you something. In 58 years of working with people all over the world, mind you, in personal development, I have never seen a person that has experienced the growth that you've experienced, in a relatively short period of time. There is a present maturity that is very obvious. You have become an absolutely incredible leader, and by a person's fruit you will know them. You must always give credit where credit is due. You're doing a phenomenal job.

There isn't an organization in the world that wouldn't be proud to have you on their executive team, to watch you make it happen. And that's really where it's at, Alex.

I consider it an honor to be a friend of yours, I really do. I like seeing people make things happen, fast and in a big way. That is the whole story of my life.

All I've attempted to do is work with people who do that: "make things happen fast and in a big way."

There is one thing I'm sure of, Alex. You have taken one or two small steps in the direction of greater things. You are going to continue doing great things, many of which are beyond your wildest dreams. You probably don't see it right now — although you may be planning on it — it will be an incredible journey.

Remember, it all happens here, Alex: In the mind.

Your Friend,
Bob Proctor

CONTENTS

Introduction   1

Part One   4

1. Build With Passion   5
2. Framing Your Foundation   13
3. Your Ultimate Potential   19
4. Experts and Entertainers   29
5. Stand Strong in the Storm   39
6. The Marvelous and Miraculous Mind   51

Part Two: A New Way of Thinking   60

7. The Foundation of Achievement   65
8. Follow Through and Stay Disciplined   75
9. The Most Successful Game   83
10. Ethics of Success   89
11. Follow One Course Until Successful   99
12. God's Greatest Gift: The Imagination   107

Part Three: Final Remarks   112

13. Above All Else, Love Deeply!   113
14. Life, Legacy, and The Pursuit of Greatness   123
15. Alive   129

Conclusion. . . In Loving Memory of Bob Proctor   139

Author's Bio   141

INTRODUCTION

Every person who exists has a great opportunity to WIN in life. WIN refers to all areas of our lives. I have written this book to bridge the gap between where you currently are and where you truly want to be. I have included stories and lessons that I have learned along my journey, and I have done my best to give you the knowledge in a way that you can apply to your own life. Your health, wealth, relationships, growth, and overall happiness are essential to you living a great and fulfilling life.

Page by page and chapter by chapter, this book will serve as a tool to help you decide what success means to you. It is intended to help you think differently about some of the challenges you may encounter as you pursue greater things in your life. I hope that as you read this book and take in the stories I have included, you will begin to ask yourself some deeper and more meaningful questions that help you to find your *Why*. You will learn about principles and laws that work in synchronicity with your mind to attract the people and places you need to get to where you want to go. You will discover endless possibilities for an elevated way of thinking and doing in your life.

A purpose-driven and fulfilling life is strikingly similar to a puzzle scattered all over the floor, waiting for you to assemble it. You already have the shapes, sizes, colors, and pieces in front of you, and you simply need to figure out how to put it all together.

As you read this book, you will realize how powerful you already are. I'm not providing you with new information on success. I'm simply putting it all together so anybody can fully understand it. Back in 2011, when I first got hold of this information, my entire life changed. I was completely dumbfounded to realize its simplicity. I'm not saying success is easy. But it is simple. Everything operates by law. When we live our lives and grow our businesses by universal laws, everything seems to play out to our benefit

When we don't, however, success can seem like a million miles away.

I've traveled all over the world, speaking in over 70 countries, earning well over $50 million by the time I was 31 years old, and I am a big believer that people truly want more out of life, but are simply unaware how to get it. People don't earn $100,000 a year because they want to. They earn $100,000 a year because they aren't aware of how to earn $100,000 a month. This book is about turning our dreams into everyday realities.

That may sound too good to be true, but it is, in fact, true. I'm living proof of this, and I'm going to give you the step-by-step blueprint to help you manifest all that you desire.

As you hold this book, I believe you have in your hands what you've been searching for. You've attracted this moment into your life. This book is meant to be in your hands, and I am your mentor. The same way the universe had me meet my mentor, Bob Proctor, at a water fountain outside an event in North Carolina, is the same way the universe is connecting you and your dreams to this book.

Each chapter of this book holds immense value, special information that you must learn and apply in order to achieve success. The ideas in this book have been tested through the decades by thinkers like Andrew Carnegie, Napoleon Hill, Earl Nightingale, and Bob Proctor. Personally, over the last almost 11 years, I've seen these philosophies and ideas help over 1,000 individuals from all walks of life create incomes of $100,000 a year, $100,000 a month, $100,000 a week, and even millions a month for some. I call that *extraordinary* results!

Here is an example. I've helped individuals from Central America, with no formal education or resources, springboard to incomes of $50,000 and even $250,000 a month. Others, who had major mental and personal issues that had led them to be unhappy, were completely transformed into happy and productive individuals. Now it's your turn to put this information to the test in your life.

Think about what you want. Applying these ideas, changing your thinking, and operating differently will bring you what you want. Since 2011, anything I've wanted I have received. The same can be true for you.

Your goal as you read through these chapters is to increase your awareness to a higher level. As your awareness expands and increases, you will awaken to the truth that you are God's highest form of creation, capable of achieving anything you desire. Pretty amazing stuff, right?

I fell in love with these ideas and information. I'm obsessed with helping people to wake up and discover how powerful they truly are. Everyone who reads, learns, and applies this information has the potential to attract and enjoy a much higher standard of overall living. Better health, much more money (in fact, multiple streams of income), deeper and more fulfilling relationships, and a purposeful, meaningful life. We are all truly God's highest form of creation; we achieve great things, and we make this world a better place.

Before you begin your journey, let me warn you that merely reading and memorizing this book will not guarantee that you make it happen in your life. You must fully understand and apply the ideas and philosophies you find here in your everyday life. Think deeply and carefully about the ideas in this book. They are simple to understand, but it will take time to burn into your subconscious mind and your soul.

Keep this book with you, continually read it, study it, and apply its teachings. Everybody's birthright is to become RICH and live a significant life. Let's get started on yours right now. I hope you enjoy your journey to your new way of living.

Dream big,

Alex Morton

Part I

BUILD WITH PASSION

"If you have a strong purpose in life, you don't have to be pushed. Your passion will drive you there." – Roy T. Bennett

When I was 18 years old, I knew a young man with a promising future.

He was ambitious, intelligent, good-humored, and full of potential. The problem was that he had no clear-cut goals that would direct him to a well-designed future of passion and purpose. If you sat him down and asked him what he wanted from life, he would have given you an ill-defined version of an idea he had thought little about. He was a personable guy, destined to be the life of the party if you caught him on a good night.

He attended Arizona State University, which is one of the most reputable schools in the nation. Most of the students lucky enough to attend ASU did one of two things: They worked hard and graduated with a well-earned degree, or they did what my friend did: "He majored in minor things," as Jim Rohn (entrepreneur, author, motivational speaker) might suggest.

Many people lack a clear understanding of what building a vision for the future looks like. College certainly does not teach this. In fact, most educational institutions conveniently shy away from any worthy teaching geared toward cultivating a life of success. After graduating high school, the primary aim is to choose a major, enroll in the required course curriculum, and then graduate with a degree. For some graduating high school students, applying to different schools is a big deal. When they get accepted to their school of choice, it's an even bigger deal.

I knew a lot of students on campus who took their acceptance into a school like ASU seriously, but not the young man in this story. If you caught him at the end of the night, which campus police sometimes did, he likely had about 12 to 15 shots of hard liquor in his system. Apart from his reckless behavior, which usually occurred up to five nights a week, he got up the next day and repeated his usual pattern.

Aside from attending his regular classes, he was involved in the real estate industry. Working part-time, going to school, and partying six nights a week eventually caught up with him. After several repeat offenses and a compounding effect of compromising behavioral patterns, the bright light inside this 18-year-old student grew dim. The university threatened to expel him following an arsenal of citations from campus police and local Tempe authorities. His GPA was suffering terribly, and the negligent behavioral patterns eventually took a toll on his relationships and his self-esteem.

You might think that a young man like this needs no introduction. We usually make that sort of assumption about the people we place on a pedestal with enormous amounts of success. People like Steve Jobs and Elon Musk. The story above is less than appealing to those who strive for greatness. Some might even argue that the behavior described is indicative of a person who will surely fail most of their life. Why would anyone tell a story that nobody wants to hear about? It's simple! To understand what makes people successful, you also need to understand what cultivates a life of failure.

It is worth noting that failure is inevitable, but if the behaviors that lead to failure persist, they become patterns. These patterns will eventually become problems.

IT'S NOT ROCKET SCIENCE!

The English mathematician Isaac Newton is widely recognized for his work in physics, mathematics, and science. He remains influential because of his contributions surrounding the laws of the universe. I am no expert on physics, science, or mathematics. I did, however, study the principles of success. I found that Isaac Newton not only revolutionized the science of the universe, but gave us some practical ways we can look at success.

Newton identified three laws of motion (an object at rest remains at rest, an object in motion remains in motion at constant speed, and there is an equal and opposite reaction for every action). You may be most familiar with the third. For our purposes, it could be phrased as, "For every success habit, there is an equal and opposite pattern that follows." One of the ways we define success is the attainment of your desired outcome. Failure is the result of mismanaged priorities. Both success and failure are predicated on the things you do day in and day out on a consistent basis.

You might consider Newton's work through the law of polarity, which decrees that everything has an opposite side of the spectrum. With that in mind, I would like to discuss the things that may be occupying most of your time. Most people have a sort of passion or something they are innately drawn to. In many instances, these things can become obsessions. Obsession should not be assumed to be a negative thing. It is, however, our obligation to make sure we channel our obsessions into a positive experience. When nourished properly, the result will fulfill your purpose.

I believe that this is a primary component for becoming outrageously successful in whatever you choose to do. Your job is to make an honest evaluation of where you are now and what your life will look like if you continue to follow your current formula.

This formula comprises your beliefs, thoughts, emotions, and your actions. What are you currently building for yourself? You've heard it quoted many times, "Without a vision, people perish." What does your vision look like? Is the foundation or belief that you're building a sturdy one? Are the tools (thoughts and emotions) you're working with constructive or dull? Could your building technique (actions) be improved?

"fixer-upper"

FROM REAL ESTATE TO REALITY CHECK

I opened this with the story of a young man who had a lot of potential and who was inhibited by mismanaged priorities.

The foolish college student was yours truly.

I was blissfully unaware of where I was heading. I knew that I would be successful, and I knew it was possible to rise above my mediocre mindset patterns. I realized that the story I had been telling had no substantial value to my life or the lives of others. There was hardly any substance that I could leverage to begin cultivating success in every area of my life.

I decided at a young age that I wanted to make a difference in the world. At that particular point in time, I lacked only the understanding of how I would make that happen. I was merely going through the motions, working part-time in real estate, and getting through school in the most lackluster, foolish way.

I can recall the first time I closed a real-estate deal. My commission check was probably $700, but man, I was excited! I thought it would be a good idea to party until 6 a.m., knowing my dad was picking me up to take me to the closing of the deal the next morning. I got a little hasty about celebrating the wins. I woke up the next day and made my way to the rental car my dad had arrived in. At that time, my parents were still living in Ohio.

Now, my parents deserve a real introduction. They are the best examples of integrity, love, and work ethic — not to mention always incredibly supportive of me and my younger sister, Maddie. My dad understood that my first deal was a big deal to me, and he traveled from Ohio to Arizona to show his support. As I made my way to the passenger seat of the car, he took one whiff of me and said, "Holy shit, Alex, you smell like booze! Go upstairs and change your clothes." I will never forget the feeling I had. All children have a conscious or an unconscious desire to make their parents proud of them. Nothing can disrupt your pattern and kill your pride like that of a parent or a loved one who is utterly disappointed in you.

build a firm foundation

That moment taught me that passion focused on the wrong priorities results in pain. Passion, obsession, or addiction can each result in an opposing outcome, much as seen in Newton's third law, and the concept demonstrated in the Law of Polarity. There are healthy passions and unhealthy passions. The same can be said of obsessions and addictions. Your passion can be a vehicle that steers you to your purpose, or a vehicle that steers you to your problems. Obsessions can help cultivate drive, and they can also be destructive. Addiction, which also has its negative connotation, can be a vehicle that accelerates people just as fast as it can cause people to spiral.

Most things in life work as a double-edged sword. Understanding which side of the blade you work with is important. Healthy passions, obsessions, and addictions are often compatible with success. Unhealthy involvement in the wrong things can be the blade edge that cuts you. I knew that if I wanted to become successful and really make it to the top, I had to rearrange my priorities and become addicted to the right things.

I became obsessed with learning about the patterns, disciplines, and beliefs that frame a life of success. I took all the passion I had for the wrong things, and I began investing in the right things. Your healthy obsessions are some of the most valuable tools you can utilize when building the life of your dreams.

FIX AND FLIP YOUR FUTURE

Early last year, my wife and I began working on the blueprints for the dream home we are building for our future family. Building a home is no small undertaking. The same can be said about purchasing an old home and deciding you are going to fix it up.

As we worked out the details and fine-tuned the designs we wanted to implement into the new house, the process led me to discover that building your dream life is a lot like building a dream home. Renovating an older home or taking on a fixer-upper project is comparable to personal growth. There is nothing easy about it. When working on an older build, you may run into structural damages that can compromise the entire process. Similarly, when you decide you want to make some changes in your life, you may have to address some old behavioral patterns that go back to a foundational level.

Sometimes, your problems in creating a new thinking process are because you are working against an old belief system. Many readers of this book have found it easy to fall back into a pattern of thinking, "It's easier said than done!" You're right! Growth takes a lot of work, and much like a renovation project, you will continuously come across obstacles and challenges.

The truth of the matter and the reason I wrote this book is that too many people desperately want to find the power of "It's already done!"

"from 'I want to' TO 'ALL IN' TO 'It's done!'

without doing the work. This is a phrase that developed from my passion and my obsession with understanding success and helping others to create it in their lives, too. It's a conviction that I can stand upon with unwavering belief because I built my life from that place on a foundational level.

My goal is to teach you that personal growth is more than a fresh paint job you slap on the walls of an old home. I want you to build your success on a firm foundation. When the storms of life come – and trust me, they will – I want you to have the confidence that what you've built will not be shaken.

As you read the chapters that follow, I want you to assess the blueprint you have of your current life. I want you to evaluate some of the older patterns that may be problematic. Some of you need a full renovation of your current reality, and with the right tools, I believe it's possible! I want you to go ALL IN as you read this book and begin implementing the strategies in your own life. I want you to get passionate and obsessed about framing your future. I want you to examine the concepts throughout this book and be honest about the areas of your life that they may apply to. It's time to flip your failures and move forward. Think about the things you want to accomplish. Think about the people you want to help. Begin at once to develop the desires that will aid in designing your life. Get passionate about your life project! Become addicted to adding to your life and the lives of others! If I can do it, you can, too! It's already done!

FRAMING YOUR FOUNDATION

"Whatever we plant in our minds and nourish with repetition and emotion will one day become a reality." – Earl Nightingale

In early 2011, when I began to develop my passion for studying success, I noticed a distinct quality that separated the ultra-successful from those who were content to fall into a life of mediocrity.

Success is more than a disciplined way of living your life. It is a disciplined way of thinking about your life. It's a perspective from which you evaluate your life's circumstances.

I realized that every stereotype surrounding the ideal of success is shallow in comparison to the depths discovered as a person moves toward the attainment of their dreams. Taking that first step unfolds layers of awareness about your life that take the average person decades to discover.

We have been disillusioned to think that successful people and those inclined to fail are on opposite sides of the spectrum. While they may have polarizing outcomes, this is not true. Sometimes failure is the result of too much involvement in the wrong things, as I explored in the opening chapter. Other times, it can result from not enough involvement in the right things. It can be caused by acting with one foot in and one foot out. Successful people simply find gratification in going to the depths that most are not willing to go to. They understand that to finish what you start is the ultimate reward. When they set out to achieve something, they do so with an attitude of assurance. An assurance that shifts, "I want to do" to "It's already done." They have made up their minds, and there is resolution and major results following the commitment. Being successful means understanding the nature of what it is like to go ALL IN.

SHARPEN YOUR AX

In my study of success, I spent a lot of my time reading books from many great pioneers of success. Some of the leading success literature often mentions Abraham Lincoln. Among other achievements, Lincoln is known for his life wisdom: *"Give me six hours to chop down a tree and I will spend the first four sharpening the ax."* Something tells me that he knew the value of a tool when placed in the hands of a person who knows how to use it.

I mentioned that my wife and I are in the process of building our new home. This requires much more than skilled construction workers. While some projects can be done quickly with the right team, the establishment of our home will also require the right tools and the right equipment. With the proper tools in the hands of people who know how to use them, the building, framing, and foundation will be firmly established to cater to our family and the experiences that will make our house a home.

Since we are examining constructing your life, it's important to understand the importance of not only being aware of your tools, but how to use them. Your primary tool as a builder will not be found at a home improvement store alongside cutting saws and framing guns. You were born with the essential tools and equipment to navigate throughout the various seasons of life. Your mind is and will remain the primary tool you use to build and maintain a successful life. As you discover how to leverage this tool, you will learn that there are no shortcuts. If you desire to be effective on your journey, you must learn how to master the machinery you are working with. You must learn how to master your mindset. Success, as Abraham Lincoln put it, is sharpening your ax while everybody else rushes to remove the objects in front of them. It is disciplining your mind, taking hold of your thoughts, and recognizing the direction that they are leading you. To truly understand this is to gain confidence that outlasts the complications of life.

THE UNEXAMINED MIND BREEDS UNDESIRED RESULTS

I have learned much about success by traveling the world. My wife and I have shared several unforgettable experiences, one of my personal favorites being Greece. Apart from the beautiful scenery, Greece has incredible culture and history. We still look to many of its ancient philosophers for wisdom. One of the most extraordinary remains Socrates, born in Athens.

Socrates said, "The unexamined life is not worth living." Consider what he meant: Whatever we can see in our minds, we can surely hold in our hands. If your life is preceding the pattern of your primary thought processes, the question to ask is, "Where are my thoughts taking me?" Examine your thoughts. Think about what you are thinking about. A lot of philosophy has been built on principles and ideas that were taught in sacred writings such as, "Bring every thought into captivity." If you could care less about philosophical teachings, and you have a thing for the scriptures; that one is for you! If you prefer science, I've dropped a few examples for you, too. What I am getting at is this: Learning how to master your mind and your thoughts is universally known to be the most powerful skill you can acquire.

I don't care about your Myers Briggs personality score, your zodiac sign, or your enneagram number. The depth of your life has nothing to do with which category you fall into, nor does your IQ score, or your grade point average. Success has nothing to do with any of these things. Categories can be dangerous. They can insidiously keep you trapped inside your comfort zone. They allow you to create stories about who you are and why you do what you do.

When you identify with such stories, they reinforce any excuses you may have for not creating the changes you need to make. If you wish to build your life, you must examine what you are working with and, in many cases, what you are working against. Stories can put you in a box, kind of like a prison cell with no bars. The only way to get outside of those boxes is to expand your perimeters.

No argument suggests life is easy. While that may seem obvious, people often act in a way that would suggest otherwise. They live with the grass-is-greener-elsewhere mentality. No matter the condition, excuses make a case for their lack of conviction. The quickest way to delay any kind of build is to remain in a state of blame. I'm sorry to break it to you, but the vibrancy of your lawn doesn't depend on the conditions of life, and it certainly has nothing to do with anyone else. If your life seems to be a little dry and withered, start by checking your mental nutritional intake. What are you feeding your mind? If your thoughts were the water that gives life to the field in front of you, have you stopped to check the system?

Polluted thoughts are like toxic water. They can never sustain you, and eventually the lack of purity becomes the primary source of your problems. Everything begins in your mind. Your mind will aid in the development of your dream life just as fast as it can destroy your destiny. When we control our thoughts and feelings, we become the creators of our physical experience here on Earth.

PERFECTION KILLS PERFORMANCE

It has taken me a little over two years to write this book, but it took me over a decade of experience to grasp how powerful the mind truly is. Admittedly, the passion I have for the ideas in this book continues to evolve. My life is a work in progress. This is true for every person I have ever met.

Building your dream life is a project that will persist until the day you leave this world behind. The good news is that you are the project manager. You play a fundamental role throughout the entire process. Perfection is not the goal, and it is not the destination. If you constantly strive to be perfect, it will become a limitation. I say this not to discourage you, but to emphasize the importance of building up skills like repetition, dedication, and adaptation.

Repetition is what fortifies the foundation for success. Dedication is a disciplined state that you practice despite how you feel. It opposes every excuse that holds you back from fulfilling your goals. Adaptation is a necessary skill that will help you to navigate the obstacles in life. It allows you to pivot when things don't go as planned.

Nobody is perfect, despite what their social media accounts claim. We all confront problems. Trials exist for everyone, and that's not just a cliché to motivate you to keep pushing through. It's the truth, yet millions of people succumb to sinister thinking patterns of shame, guilt, confusion, and inferiority. Why? The thing is, we live in a society that has cultivated the expedited experience. This experience is artificial at best, and it thrusts people into false hope.

People get looped into thinking that if they buy the program, take the e-course, compound all the techniques from success literature, and yet they don't achieve results now, there must be something wrong with them. Simultaneously, they end up reinforcing a belief in the never mentality. Throughout your life, you are telling a story. This story goes on to manifest in your physical world whether it's circumstances, relationships, economic status – you name it. The problem is that most people never realize that they control the narrative in their life. When you can't understand that you run the story, whatever story you have started to run with can eventually ruin you. The noise within our world and the news feeds within our heads have opened doors to feeling bad for ourselves, complacency, and illegitimacy.

"*Successfully tune out the world by FOCUSING*"

The real manifestations of these problems have saturated the mind, will, and emotions of many people. Instead of being wired to achieve and to progress, they have been programmed to accommodate and "fit in."

Disempowering is a gross understatement. People all over the world, of every age group and ethnicity, are silently losing battles and in turn losing their lives. We are raising a generation of young people to believe that if they don't adequately live up to unrealistic societal standards, such as the lifestyles of Instagram influencers, they are failures. Something needs to change, and change in a hurry.

If the current events headlining your story are not serving you, get a better narrative. You need to examine the thinking patterns that may be keeping you in a box that feels like a prison cell. Getting stuck is temporary. Staying stuck is a decision. Using dull tools to make progress is exhausting. Sharpen your mind. Purge the ingrained ideas of demoralizing labels that you have somehow adapted to and adopt something different.

I have heard it said that one of the first words a child will learn is no. This is a tragedy, but it does not need to become a routine. I want you to get back to the drawing board and work on the new and official blueprints of your dream life. I want you to say yes to the vision in front of you, not behind you. Fall in love with those ideas and celebrate their attainment both physically and mentally. Having and maintaining control of your mind will bring you closer to your goals. Decide what it is you truly want and decide that you're going to get it. Don't let the little voice in your head hold you back. You control your thinking. If it can work for me, it can work for you. Step into who you were born to be. As you master your mindset, you can begin to look at all the things that you want to do and say, "It's already done!"

YOUR ULTIMATE POTENTIAL

"As he thinks, so he is; as he continues to think, so he remains."
— James Allen

To change your life, you cannot rely on motivation to take you there. I believe that the reason people are often haunted by their dreams and desires is that they are not willing to part ways with some things that slow them down. The dreams and desires of your heart are intrinsically connected to who you are.

"Out of great tragedy — great heroism"

There will be many times in life where you will come face to face with distractions, whatever they may be. Distractions can be anything from an ignorant friend to a disappointment. They can be negative habits you formed as you were developing into the person you are today. One of the evil things about distractions is that, at some point in time, they may have helped you. We can say the same of bad habits, which most of the time begin as coping mechanisms to take away from the immediate pain of a situation. Maybe you were insecure in your life because you were smaller than all the other kids in your class. By no fault of your own, you may have been bullied or picked on because of a trait or a characteristic that separated you from the other kids. You then decided that in order to stop the bullying, you would spend hours in the gym, or you would change your diet. For girls, the reasons may have been looking different than the crowd, and perhaps you decided it was time to wear more makeup or change your hairstyle.

Actions can begin as coping mechanisms, and they can result in chains. Not that taking pride in your health and appearance is a bad thing, but who are you really doing it for? Psychologists have determined that our youth has shaped many of our adult behaviors. Counterfeit confidence comes from behavior modification done for the wrong reasons. There are confusing consequences that come when we seek validation from a world that values some of the most despicable things. External validation results in misleading responses that eventually lead you to conclude that who you are connected to influences how others perceive you — which, let me tell you, is nonsense.

One of the greatest success habits is tuning out the world and FOCUSING on doing what you know needs to be done for success. When you trade conviction for conformity, you chase invisible targets. Then begins the vicious cycle of addiction to the approval of others. We sow seeds of diversion when we decide to cultivate an identity that is completely inconsistent with our desires.

Failure in life begins as a slow diverting of our attention. It's dangerous because most people don't always realize it's happening until they wake up next to an empty bottle of antidepressants and most of the medicine in their cabinet have, "For Fast Relief" written on the prescription label.

The truth is that there is no fast lane to the future. You are today making the decisions that will create your tomorrow. The reason I am so passionate about what I do is that we live in a world where too many people have developed the skill of shapeshifting instead of space shifting. I don't know about you, but I want to be the person who can walk into a room and shake the atmosphere. Most people do. Unfortunately, this is rarely the case because people have been trained to conform to the pattern of their environments. The goal of this book is to teach you how to harness the power that makes you unique and to give you the confidence to walk into a room and contribute. Success is the opposite of mediocre.

Success is a disciplined effort to sow the right seeds. Success is responding to corrections with humility. It is not conforming to a cynical society. You don't wake up and say, "Today is the day that I am going to ruin my life." Nobody does that. It may appear to be a single moment, but every moment is a compounding movement within your mindset. Success is a process of what you plant and what you nourish.

THE MAN WITH THE RED BANDANA

The United States recently marked the 20th anniversary of one of the most horrific days in history. On September 11, 2001, at 8:46 a.m. ET, a hijacked American Airlines flight struck the north tower of the World Trade Center in New York City. A little over 15 minutes later, at 9:03 a.m. ET, another hijacked plane flew into the south tower of the World Trade Center. I was in the 6th grade at an elementary school in Bexley, Ohio, when the news of the attack was broadcast live to millions of families around the world. I am sure that many of you can recall exactly where you were, too.

As people watched the tragedy unfold in New York City, the catastrophic events quickly escalated, leaving millions in a state of paralyzing fear. At 9:37 a.m. ET, a third plane struck the Pentagon building in Washington, D.C., and at 10:03 a.m. ET, United Airlines flight 93 crashed in a field near Pennsylvania, resulting in the death of all passengers aboard the plane. Four hijacked planes took the lives of almost 3,000 people that day. I still get chills as I recall the memory of that day, a heavyweight that reminds us that life is fragile.

As I began reflecting on the many lives that were lost and the many lives that were forever changed, I realized that out of great tragedy also comes stories of great heroism. On the 78th floor of the south tower, people were desperately fighting the heat of flames and the heavy clouds of smoke that had saturated the building. Surrounded by wreckage and uncertain that hope would arrive, a calm voice sounded amongst survivors, "Everyone who can stand, stand now. If you can help others, do so." Nobody knew who this young gentleman was. They had not known his name, but a red bandana covered his mouth as he led people to safety.

This is the story of a young man named Welles Remy Crowder. During a dark hour, he stepped up to fight not only for his life, but for the lives of those around him. With authority and selfless ambition, he directed people to a flight of stairs while carrying a woman with him down to the 61st floor where they were met by other rescuers. He continued his mission to save lives, risking his own as he went back up to retrieve as many surviving victims as time would allow. He worked as an American Equities trader, but he had previously joined his father as a volunteer firefighter when he was 16 years old. There have been articles published on his heroism, and several documents that account for his heroism. Prior to the events that devastated the world on September 11, Welles had mentioned to his father that he was contemplating changing his career. His dad shared his son's dreams of becoming a New York City firefighter. Welles did not get the chance to switch from his career, but the opportunity to fight was one he seized. He was 24 years old when he lost his life on 9/11/2001. He led 18 people to safety before the building collapsed.

Welles is one of many heroes who stepped up to save lives on such a terrible day in history. We honor and remember several heroes among the lives lost, and we will never forget them. There are people today that live to tell the stories of the courageous men and women who impacted history by deciding to act with courage in the presence of chaos. Shortly after the twentieth anniversary of 9/11, the heroic acts of many led others to consider what they would have done. Have you ever asked yourself how you might act in the face of adversity? Have you considered what it is you would do if you knew you had limited time? Do you remember where you were on 9/11/2001?

Reflect for a moment back to a time in your life where you came face-to-face with a daunting decision. Are you a different person now? What was your friend group like? Did you have any big goals and dreams that you may have lost sight of? Life will pass you by — it pauses for nobody. In a year, in five years, ten, twenty, thirty years from now, you will arrive somewhere in your life. In seasons of conflict and confusion, it is the tendency of our mind to sort through question after question.

This tendency to make connections and find resolution is the resource you can leverage to create success.

If I interviewed you today and asked similar questions, consider that your preparation now will determine the progression of your future. Who do you want to be in the next five years, fifteen years, twenty-five years? What are you committed to in the current season that may hold you back? Have you become the person you had aspired to be in the former years? If not, how are you going to change? What do you need to do differently to secure the future of risen standards? What decisions are you making moment by moment that get you closer to or farther from your goals?

YOU NEED TO MAKE A DECISION

I was 21 years old when I determined I wanted to be a multimillionaire. At 16, I knew I wanted success, and I had even painted an abundantly clear picture of what it would look like. Five years later, I had arrived at a destination, and it certainly wasn't the Porsche Tower in Miami, FL. I was the foolish college kid I told you about in chapter one. My regular diet consisted of Taco Bell and ramen noodles for dinner. You know the story! I had no financial resources, there were no mentors in my inner circle, and the clear-cut goals I had for my future were virtually nonexistent. I knew that the person I was showing up as in my day-to-day life contradicted my character.

I had to upgrade to my ultimate potential. Within a few years, I discovered this potential and its power to transform every aspect of my life. I had to discipline myself daily, so that I would not falter every time something or someone distracted me. I decided where I would allocate my time. I took inventory of who I spent my time with. I started reading books on the power of mindset. I decided I would spend more time learning than partying. I made the decision that I would condition both my mind and my physical body to match my desired outcome.

Success is not a stage in life, it's a process of decisions that you make to take an action to produce a result. It is the belief that commitments are shallow unless met with consistency. There is no magic potion that can put you in motion toward your desired outcome. Caffeine helps to keep you awake, but there is an enormous difference between being awake and being alive. In creating lasting change, you must never rely on your feelings to fuel your footsteps. Feelings are fickle, and we can see throughout history that ultimate love, ultimate sacrifice, and ultimate potential did not rise from a feeling of empowerment. In fact, it was the *act of doing* that created the momentum needed for every significant achievement.

Momentum always follows the decision, not the other way around. "When I'm rich, I will help people in need." "When I have millions of followers and people know who I am, I will talk about the things I am passionate about." "When I am fit and healthy, I will stop annihilating my self-image."

The "When this, then that" propaganda has been programmed into our society that stops us from resolving the important ideas that we are purposed for. From a young age, commercials have normalized and cultivated the idea that you need something outside of your current circumstances to create a change. Wrong. The act of seeing things as clearly as they are, untainted by doubt and delusion, is not up for negotiation.

Decisions plus action will determine where you end up in the next decade of your life. Decide what it is you want and then take actionable steps to make it happen. When I decided I was going to revolutionize every area of my life, I started by making disciplined decisions.

The first major area that changed was my work ethic. I was waking up early and organizing my day around business. At 9:00 a.m., 11:00 a.m., 1:00 p.m., 3:00 p.m. I was clocking in the hours to build toward where I wanted my company to be. At 5:00 p.m. and 7:00 p.m. I was orchestrating and leading presentations. By 9:00 p.m., I was at team trainings. Not for one day a week or even three days a week. I was doing this daily for six years. I wanted to outwork every person in the industry, and I disciplined my actions to follow suit.

THE ROSE BUSH RECKONING

Nature is a great example of life's greatest lessons, especially those on success. I gave you an example of viewing your life regarding a landscape. I mentioned that toxic thinking is like polluted water that saturates the field in front of you. When we look at the world around us, nature is always telling a story. This is the reason we often hear nature referenced in poetry, religion, philosophy, and elsewhere. We learned that toxic water can kill good grass. In the same way, polluted ideas and toxic thinking patterns can destroy your life. This is not the only lesson that nature can teach us.

The women in my life – my mom, sister, and fiancée – love flowers. I noticed that whenever I ordered an arrangement for them, most came with a rose. I know little about plants, and I can't pretend that I would ever successfully keep them alive, but thank God for the gardeners! The roses caught my attention, not just because they looked nice and they made the people I love smile, but I was always convinced that some flowers could only be bought in season. While this is probably true for most plants, there is a reason that they often use roses in arrangements that last for a longer time. They have a unique ability to bloom in larger quantities, depending on the care they receive. There is a process known as pruning that a skilled gardener would have to do to reap the benefits of a well-kept rose garden. Pruning helps to ensure that the flowers will survive, despite a change in weather. It adds to the lifespan of the plant while enhancing the quality and quantity of roses that bloom.

"To produce a life of quality and abundance, you must prune it"

Thanks to the incredible women in my life, I learned a lesson that I found to be synonymous with success. The pruning process ensures the success of the rose bushes, and it is no small task. Evidently, pruning a bush is the act of cutting away and stripping back everything that is no longer wanted. It takes skill and knowledge to be done effectively, without damage to the entire bush. Much like the success of a rose bush, to produce a life of quality and abundance, you will need to strip away some things that no longer nourish you. You will have to cut off some things that don't fit the season of life you desire to step into. Cut off distractions. Sometimes, you will have to cut off certain relationships. You will have to prune away the problematic thinking patterns. Your decision to grow will be met with a giant pair of cutting shears, and you will need to strip away the things in your life that stop you from producing your ultimate potential.

I realized in a moment that my life would not be predicated on the occurrences I had no control over. I realized that success is a state of being that arises from being fully invested in the process. Not "interested," but "invested." There is a difference between being interested in success and being fully immersed in the process of becoming successful.

The truth I had to reconcile with is the idea that I was on the trajectory of what I would tolerate.

I would hear people complaining about going to their 9-5 jobs, and at a certain point I could empathize with the apathy, until I realized that there was no valid excuse for what we accept. You and I are responsible for the standards we set for ourselves. We can't control the circumstances or the economy, and I dare you to try to make the sun set two hours early. You can't do it, and in life you will rarely control the challenges you confront or the customers/leaders that yell at you, but you can certainly control how you manage these things.

If you don't enjoy the job you have to show up for, simply saying that you "have to" would be a fantasy. I am not advising you to put in your two weeks' notice if it's your only source of income — but you bet I am holding you accountable for what you do with the rest of your time. What decisions are you making that can change your outcome?

Your decisions and your choices will always fall in line with what you believe about yourself. Have you ever committed to something and found yourself at the mercy of your former patterns? It's probably time to pick apart the ideas that you have identified with. Humanity has an impressive ability to adapt to a belief. The thing about beliefs is that they, too, can change. Some of you need to make some decisions about the things in your life that no longer serve you.

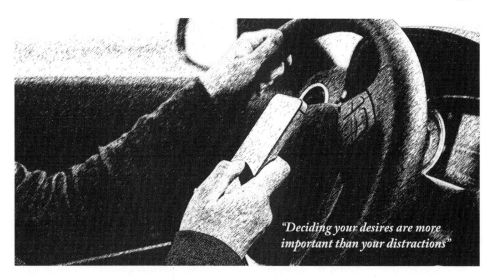

"Deciding your desires are more important than your distractions"

I, too, must overcome and adapt to challenges, and believe me, it is a daily discipline. I've got my desires, and I've got my distractions. Everyone on the planet has desires and distractions. Whatever that goal is, whatever success means to you, for you to go to that next level, your decisions will appear to be reckless and insane to those who don't understand what you are working toward. When you make that decision, there will be a reckoning that takes precedence over the defeating perspectives and patterns that are debilitating you. When you decide that your desires are more important than your distractions, that is when the magic will happen.

FOLLOW THROUGH TO FLOURISH

In pruning rose bushes, stripping away the dead and deteriorating branches can be messy. It's normal to want to cling to the familiar, but you must make an honest assessment of the areas that no longer benefit your life. The transition process that follows a decision requires a disciplined maintenance period.

This is going to look different for everyone, so don't compare your growth to that of other people. Like you, everyone has a unique starting point, and we all have different strengths and weaknesses. Focus on your fruit. Be deliberate about your daily intake. What are you listening to? What are you reading? What shows are you watching? Who are you spending your time with? What are you doing to condition your body daily? What are you doing to condition your mind? These are questions I will continue to ask throughout this book. Get used to the sort of things you should always be aware of on a day-to-day basis.

The key to success in any area of your life is to make sure that the decisions you make daily are getting you closer to the desires and dreams that you have.

Nourish your mind and your body while being intentional about what you prioritize. Set up a standard for what you wish to achieve, and discipline yourself to act in accordance with it. What good is target practice if you have nothing to aim at? You must get a clear-cut idea of what it is you want, and constantly check in to make sure you are on track. The most powerful things in life follow the decisions you make. Momentum does not come from a feeling — it comes from the decision to flourish despite harsh conditions. Flourish amid fear. Flourish in the failed attempts to make something stick. Flourish in building the right relationships and connections. Flourish in the fullness of your ultimate potential.

Deep down, there is a hero in all of us. Welles Crowder showed us what the power of a decision can do. His selfless decision during the events of 9/1/11 to put others first, saved the lives of 18 people, and affected the hearts of many more. You, too, can confront and cut away the things that hold you back from achieving your dreams and moving toward becoming the best version of yourself.

I am giving you the tools to prune what's holding you back, and I promise that if you remain patient, you will see an abundance of growth in due season. Stay committed to disciplining your mind, and your daily decisions, your hard work, will produce fruit. The compounded effort will in turn become the seed to produce your future harvest. So when you wish to plant more, you won't need to start over because the fruit of labor produces an abundance to add to what you've already done. . . . It's already done!

EXPERTS AND ENTERTAINERS

"Don't judge a man by his opinions, but by what his opinions have made of him." – Georg Christoph Lichtenberg (German physicist, 1742-1799)

Reach what you have practiced. This is the opposite of the traditional advice we hear. Most of you will be more familiar with the statement, "Practice what you preach." We hear this spoken by leaders, speakers, parents, and it's possible that even you have said it a time or two. While I can appreciate the sentiment, we know actions speak louder than words.

The Internet has become a powerful vessel of clickbait content and colorful marketing strategies. With all the information available, I'd like to discuss the value of the content you are subscribing to as it pertains to success. It is imperative that you understand the difference between entertainment and expertise. You must also evaluate the sources of your information when your growth and development are concerned.

I suggest you conduct an in-depth study of the source of your information or the person who provides it. I will explore this further later on.

What separates entertainment from education? I once overheard a conversation between a former colleague and a young couple who had just become parents. You would have assumed from the way this former colleague spoke to them that he had eight kids and four grandchildren, and his parenting advice was well founded in experience. The thing was, he had no kids and no stable relationship. I don't want you to misconstrue my observation for criticism. I am merely saying that it's easy to assume that someone is an expert, even though there is a sufficient lack of evidence. Do you see the problem? It's a terrible idea to take advice from someone who doesn't preach what they have already practiced. You wouldn't ask Tiger Woods for marital advice, and you wouldn't let Justin Bieber or Kim Kardashian perform open heart surgery. It simply doesn't make sense. "Practice what you preach" is a great punchline, but if you live by that order, the joke is on you.

'TIS THE SEASON FOR TIKTOK TRENDS

The moment something is promoted, people jump at the opportunity to be a part of it. In sports, you may call these people bandwagoners. Sports are not the only illustration of people's desire to win and be a part of a win. Social media is also a catalyst for this. I was recently shopping for my wife, picking out a few gifts for the holiday season. I went to several stores to find a specific item that has been around for years. In the past, I had no problem purchasing this item because there was plenty of stock on the shelves, especially during December. I didn't want to order online because of shipping delays. No big deal, I thought. I will just go pick it up in person. After several hours and about four different store locations, I scratched my head. I was just about ready to throw in the towel on my gift search, but I decided I would try one more location. Unfortunately, I had no luck finding the item I was searching for. It was completely out of stock. Slightly irritated and pissed off, I began shopping for something else.

A sales associate that heard about my dilemma politely made her way over with a smile on her face. She had two daughters who had also missed out on some items on their Christmas lists. She explained to me that there was perhaps a TikTok trend to blame. Evidently, a well-known public figure posted something about their favorite products for daily use. Within hours, the stores were ransacked, and every product mentioned by this celebrity was no longer available. Luckily, the woman who had overheard what I was looking for had a different recommendation. I was unsure if the product I had purchased in place of my original item was any good. I trusted the woman who helped me out. She had developed her expertise, working in her industry for well over a decade. Her knowledge and her passion for what she did eventually persuaded me to purchase something else. This is the power of influence.

Here is an example of someone preaching, or pitching, something she had knowledge of and practice with. Here is also the downside of influence: In a few brief hours following a celebrity promoting a product, people couldn't wait to get their wallets out. Our society has no problems being influenced. The question is, by whom? While influence is a remarkable trait to have if you wish to be successful, sometimes you must take a step back to analyze who and what is influencing you.

This story offers a lesson. On the one hand is a woman who's an expert, and on the other a celebrity posting something about a product she'd probably been paid to promote. Our society jumped at the recommendations of an entertainer, unlikely to do the same for someone who can educate them. Society operates often from this backward mentality. We call these people sheep. Celebrities post, influencers promote, media outlets spew propaganda, and the consumer is programmed. People's daily mental intake is leaving them starving and craving more. Entertainers put on a good show. Experts and people who are educated have something to show for.

Most of the influencers who influence you are successful because of their ability to appeal to the masses. Your ignorance fuels their financial independence. Are you paying for a performance or are you investing in progress? That is, in your progress, not theirs. Certainly not every person you look up to is pulling the wool over your eyes. There are some great resources that can help assist you and provide you with valuable information. But this kind of content is scarce. Most of what people consume daily leaves them with an insatiable hunger for more. If you're starving your mind, you can almost guarantee it will come at the cost of your success. If what you feed your mind is of any value, there will be evidence from where it comes and instruction for where it goes. You can consume all day, digesting nothing at all. Instruction is not the equivalent of "Believe what you can achieve." It is not slogans that make people successful, it is knowledge applied. It is calculated decision making about who you listen to and how you proceed with what you listen to. Make sure that the people you take advice from are preaching what they have put into practice consistently.

ROLE MODELS ROLE PLAY. MENTORS MAKE IT HAPPEN

One of the core secrets to success is to have a mentor.

Some people believe a mentor is someone you model your behaviors after. But that's not a mentor – that's a role model. They are not the same thing. Some skeptics claim that mentorship is a glorified idea that has led people astray. I have heard that mentorship even prevented some from reaching their true potential. There is too much emphasis placed on being the duplicate of someone else. Context is important, however. A great mentor never aims to clone himself or herself. They coach based on knowledge gained and applied.

An ideal mentor is a person who has gained the experience to qualify them as an expert. Entertainers, on the other hand, talk about experiences that they have not walked through. They can role-play in a reality they have never experienced. These are often the people behind the get-rich-quick schemes. They are super good at organizing and compiling the information and strategies from people who did the work. They draw you in with clickbait. Congratulations, you just paid an arm and a leg for a well-articulated e-course that was probably counterproductive. You knew better, but you didn't do better.

I want you to understand that if this sounds like you, that's ok! You're already getting better if you're gradually reading more books and fewer social media posts.

Let's go back to building your dream life. Imagine hiring somebody to sketch up a draft image based on ideas and details you share. The person doing the sketch may do a really great job on the assignment. They may even inspire you to go through with the next steps in development. While the person drafting the picture may have artistic abilities, they aren't the builder. When it comes to taking what you imagine and implementing that with strategy and skill, you need someone who understands the process. A visionary can excite you and they can strike an emotional chord, but it ends there. Inspiration without intellect is merely entertainment.

Entertainers are good at putting on a show, but they can't show you anything. They can flaunt the things they have going for them, but they can't flip your ideas or speed up your future. Building your dream life can quickly become a futile and frustrating process, leaving you feeling stuck in phase one of development.

Now what? When you find someone who has achieved what you want by putting in the necessary steps, you have found an expert.

An influencer with monetary evidence is the equivalent of a stone statue. Great reminders they may be, but success is a reality. It is not an Instagram post or a TikTok reel. It is real life with real people doing real work to create a real outcome. Having the right mentors can help you make the right decisions. Having the wrong mentors can lead you to a defeated destiny, or worse. Improper coaching can inhibit you from taking any action at all.

I have no desire to trash the people who don't agree with a lot of the success logic. In all sincerity, I believe we can learn something from every person we cross paths with. In most cases, we are learning from mistakes.

Behind every expert, there is execution.

But mentorship is not about making sure everything you do is done right. It's about making sure that nothing stops you from getting it done. It's learning from the people who have succeeded because they never let their excuses stand in the way of execution. Mentorship taught me how to prune the rose bushes, where to plant my seeds, and how to grow the abundance of fruit I have seen in my life. I believe it can do the same for you.

DON'T GIVE ME YOUR OPINIONS — SHOW ME YOUR OUTCOMES!

One of the biggest reasons most people we know – our friends, family, and coworkers – are broke, busted, disgusted, and lost in life, is because they are listening to the wrong people.

When you get into conversations, especially regarding the topics you are passionate about, you must leave no room for a person to impose their doubts on your dreams. When I was sitting down to write this book, I took a moment to compile a list of all the books that affected me most. At the top of that list, I wrote Think and Grow Rich by Napoleon Hill. In this book, Hill says, *"Opinions are the cheapest commodities on earth. Everyone has a flock of opinions ready to be wished upon anyone who will accept them. If you are influenced by 'opinions' when you reach DECISIONS, you will not succeed in any undertaking."*

"Talk is cheap – show me the evidence"

Talk is cheap. With success, there is a lot more to see than there is to say. The best people to learn from are those who let the evidence in their lives do the talking.

Everybody has a point of reference they speak from. When I began my journey at 21 years old, I learned that opinions and outcomes often tell completely different stories. I learned this from a man who has been very influential in my life, a man I can proudly call my mentor. Bob Proctor, one of the greatest teachers, thought leaders, and pioneers in his area, taught me how to read results. He taught me how to study and what to study as it pertains to success. Over the course of his 86 years (he passed away in February 2022), he studied the techniques and the attitudes of some of the most influential people in the world. He was not only one of the most valuable mentors in my life, but he, too, was mentored by several remarkably successful people.

Can you notice the pattern? Some say that success leaves clues, and I believe that if you can get around successful people, they will cue you in. Whom do you listen to? Whom do you take advice from? Who is in your ear? What music are you listening to? Whom do you allow to influence you? What accounts do you follow on social media? Whoever you've been taking advice from until this point in your life has had a great deal to do with your success or lack thereof. Before you adhere to the advice of people around you, make sure they speak from an outcome instead of an opinion.

STUDY THE STORIES

You need to study people who are successful. If you are reading this book hoping you'll charm your following with some fabricated hate speech directed at the nature of what I talk about, then have at it. Either way, you are studying someone and something. For what purpose is none of my business. Most of you have either heard of or adopted delusional idealities or ridiculous societal/cultural programming tactics. This has been going on since the time you were a kid. One of my favorite misconstrued statements would have to be, "Money is the root of all evil." In writing this book, I took into consideration that I too must be diligent in my approach to articulate a message that I have spent the time trying to understand. I must do my best to preach what I have practiced, which brings me to the topic of study. Since people like to take things out of the original context, I wanted to begin with the statement I had listed above.

I also heard that money was the root of evil. I went to the original source to further see where this idea could have come from. My parents did not teach me such things, but as a kid, you run into all kinds of contradicting life advice. From what I gathered, in the scriptures it is originally stated, *"The love of money is the root of all kinds of evil. And some people, craving money, have wandered from their true faith and pierced themselves with many sorrows"* (1 Tim. 6:10).

Somehow, this got simplified into a saying that framed wealth as an evil thing. To say that money is evil would be deliberately untrue if you further study the original source, which conveys that just to make money, an idol would leave you with a broken spirit. This I cannot contest. I have always said that money can't buy happiness, and I stand by that. Only the person who takes the time to understand something can be critical, and with good intention. Anything less would be arrogance.

Another great example of poorly established paradigms is a story many of you will be familiar with. Maybe you were told to become a doctor, lawyer, or a world-class engineer if you really wanted to earn big money. You were told to monitor your GPA, since that was the only way you could get into a good college. From there, you would graduate, find a company with good healthcare benefits, and plenty of opportunity to climb the corporate ladder. And maybe, just maybe, you would get a high-level management position.

Do you see anything wrong with this picture? Maybe not! After all, if it looks good, sounds good, and pays the bills, it must be good. Wrong! In fact, most schools will teach you about all the historical people who revolutionized change in a big way, but do they tell you how? Did you learn about the man behind the light bulb? Good old Thomas Edison, who never had a drawn-out formal education. Of course you know about Thomas Edison, but did you know that much of what led him to the discovery of electricity was through personal study? In other words, personal development.

Chances are that your school system would not have taught you this, because it wouldn't be of any benefit to them for you to know that. You would have had to study his story. This is what people like Napoleon Hill did. His entire book, Think and Grow Rich, came about because he dedicated his life to studying the lives of hundreds of the world's most successful people. We do not reserve success for the sophisticated collegiate or the talented athlete. Success is, once again, a state of being that is studied, practiced, and progressive. If you want to be successful, study success.

EXPERT OR ENTERTAINER?

Suppose you had to have a major surgery, and the doctor gave you the choice of having either Justin Bieber do the surgery or the world's leading expert in that surgical technique. That's a pathetic proposal and an idiotic scenario. The obvious choice would be the expert. Yet if you think about it, we live in a society where it is all too easy to follow the suggestions of anyone on your social media. Our culture screams that conformity is the universal approach to fulfillment. But if you wouldn't trust a celebrity with a scalpel and some anesthetic, then why would you allow people on a platform to pick you apart and put you back together again?

"Choose an expert – or an entertainer?!!!"

You may be studying a story, but is it pushing you forward or holding you back? How important is your story?

I want you to think about these things. Make a list of things you want for your future. Take it a step further and write out the dreams you have for your family. I know I want my children to have a nice family meal in front of them each night versus serving up boxed cereal several nights a week. I am impartial about breakfast for dinner, but to have no choice is a problem. That's typical for the type of person who would rather play now and work later. Also, it's another tactic of a system designed to keep people in debt. I worked hard when I was 21, and a decade later I am enjoying the benefits of that hard work. I plan to teach my children the same.

I know what I want for my wife, my family, and our future. I know it means that I must get around people who have already decided the outcome of my life. I don't need a forecasted opinion trying to depict my seasons. There will always be habits, mentalities, and disciplines that are synonymous with success. You must research them and program them through repetition.

Your career may entail sales, whether it's life insurance policies, million-dollar homes, or products through build-and-scale sales organizations—

it's all the same. Be intentional about who you take advice from. Study yourself and know what influences you, who influences you, and where that is taking you. Listen to people who have been where you desire to go. Take advice from experts.

Stop living your life for the entertainment of an audience that isn't paying attention to you. Focus on what it is you want and find the people who will help you achieve these things. Those are the criteria you need to have on your checklist before you allow anybody to scribble their ideas on the blueprints of your master design.

Family is no exception to the rule. Just because you share the same bloodline or pledged "till death do us part" at the altar, you are not obligated to give up your future to the suggestions of other people. Study people's success stories. Find a mentor who got good at narrating the book while playing the main character. Find someone who had an exceptional blueprint and still built it better. I have found there's a distinct energy involved when you study an icon when they are just developing into a superstar. Study their mindset from ten years back. Study their practices PRE their Hall of Fame speech, PRE their Powerhouse Speaker award, PRE their NYT Bestseller achievement. Study their journey and find their success trail. Practice now so that when you preach or teach others about what to do with their lives, your life is the evidence of what has already been done — that success formula you're teaching about has clearly, plainly already been done!

STAND STRONG IN THE STORM

"Celebrate your success and stand strong when adversity hits,
for when the storm clouds come in the eagles soar while the small birds
take cover." – Napoleon Hill

At the start of 2020, the entire world was affected by the Coronavirus pandemic from COVID-19. Although the virus was dominating headlines, 2020 will go down as a historical year for several other reasons. In what seems like the blink of an eye, people were hurled into a tumultuous season of life, accompanied by many storms. From pandemic to politics, the highs and lows taught us some powerful lessons about life — especially the storms of life. We learned a lot about faith, and we learned even more about what happens to a society in the absence of it. It was a challenging year for everyone, and the reigning state of mind seemed to be that of fear. People were apprehensive and pressed by the weight of adversity. The storms seemed relentless, and the seasons felt as if they morphed into one long and drawn out winter.

"Are you strong enough to stand any storm?"

By now, I hope you realize that the storms I am talking about are not the storms we hear about on the weather channel. The storms I am talking about are the ones that bring destruction to your psychological state, as well as to the state of your spirit. I have found that we can avoid a lot of pain by understanding these storms, and learning how to discern each season.

SUCCESS IN THE STORM

Most of life's metaphorical storms will not appear on your doppler radar. The intensity of the storms is subjective to varying degrees. One of these is like climate, and another is condition. In this regard, climate can be likened to the phase of life you are currently walking through, whether it's a new job, a new relationship, a challenge you may be facing, etc.

The climate of your life is essentially the primary state of emotion that you operate from. Climate is synonymous with the conscious mind, which we will explore later.

The condition of your life is the reigning state of mind that triggers your actions or your responses to the climate. The condition is linked to your subconscious, which we will also explore further on.

For you to be successful, it is imperative that you understand your climate and condition.

When you understand these, you will learn how to discern the seasons of your life. You will endure different seasons regardless of your climate or your condition. These seasons will produce storms, also unrelated to climate or condition. This is life. Your success is predicated on how well you manage yourself in each storm, and how aware you are of each season. Regardless of the origin or the nature of these storms, people have the unique ability to choose how they are going to respond. There are two kinds of storms I want to focus on. These are the event-driven storms and the belief-driven storms.

Event-driven storms arise from external conflicts. They are stirred up by politics, religious reforms, family disputes, economic affairs, or global pandemics like the one our world experienced at the beginning of 2020. When an event-driven storm causes a frenzy within our society, we see the devastating implications of improper thinking patterns. We see the dangers of a noisy world that lacks a sound perspective.

Obscurity leads the masses to a state of feeling overwhelmed. Only those who have trained themselves to remain objective amid a storm will gain an advantage. When you examine how a successful person thinks, you will find a determined effort to train the mind through the trials. There can be no triumph without trial.

Somebody who knows how to think has worked hard to develop skill sets like perceptiveness, practicality, discernment, and good judgment. They can teach you how to handle a storm and they can more or less tell you about what season it arrived. Good thinkers are always in demand, because very few people think. Psychologists have determined that the average person experiences upwards of 6,000 thoughts a day. I have often wondered how many of those thoughts are original. Where are those thoughts coming from? How many of us are relying on other people to make moral decisions for the sake of our personal well-being?

"No triumph without trials"

There is a terrible disconnect in a society that is content with dysfunctional thinking patterns. It is a tragedy when people become more susceptible to conformity and control, instead of being creative and constructive. In 2020, there was not only talk of inflation and mass shutdowns, but also worry about a lack of resources, such as building supplies. Ironically, the building supplies for developing new infrastructures weren't the only things that people lacked. The development of dreams, aspirations, goals, and vision also came to a mass halt. We should permit nothing to hinder our dreams, yet I wonder — how does your thinking change when headlines come out? Where do you position your perspective when the storm clouds roll in?

KEEP YOUR HEAD IN THE CLOUDS

I have spent a lot of time in the clouds, literally and figuratively. What I do has blessed me with the opportunity to fly all over the world. Flying is not my favorite thing to do. I never enjoyed it, especially when the pilot would announce over the speaker that there may be some turbulence. "Please remain seated with your seatbelts fastened," they say. Yeah, right! Then comes the first impact of an air pocket, and my mind immediately flees all forms of rational thinking. If it carries on long enough, anyone who may be seated around me is concerned. Not for their well-being, but whether this crazy person sitting across from them may or may not lose consciousness. All jokes aside, turbulence is not my thing. Flying, however, has served as a good analogy for life in its turbulent seasons. Although travel amid the pandemic was difficult, I was fortunate enough to not have been affected as badly as some.

I can recall a time when the news of the virus was still fresh, and my wife and I were traveling overseas for an event I was speaking at. We were traveling through some clouds and, whatever land there was beneath us, we could not see. There were many things I was probably thinking, but despite my dislike of flying, I was at peace. While the headlines were inducing fear throughout the world, we were completely disconnected from the noise. We were flying at a higher altitude somewhere between where we had taken off and the destination to which we would arrive.

I wanted to use this story to illustrate to you that sometimes thinking as successful people do, requires a disconnect from the noise. It requires you to rise above the surface of whatever is taking place, and get into a place of higher altitude. Sometimes, the best place to be in the middle of a storm is in the clouds. When you and I elevate our thinking, we can see beyond the chaos. Successful people have trained themselves to think at higher altitudes.

I am not saying that you have to get on a plane and travel across the world to get a different perspective. In fact, you can decide wherever you are to put your head in the clouds. Good thinkers solve problems, orchestrate solutions, build and conquer. They do so by bringing their attitude for life to a higher altitude.

Have you ever been daydreaming about something, and then told to get your head out of the clouds? I know I have. Back when I was in school, this was actually quite a common occurrence. If I had known what I know now, perhaps I would have responded politely by saying, "Actually, it's quite nice up here."

The only reality that you and I can control is the reality within our minds. Our thinking patterns form our perception of life. That is the primary message of this entire book. All the most successful thinkers I know spend their best efforts focusing only on what they can control. They disconnect from the patterns of society, and they elevate their thoughts. They rise above the noise, and they position their thinking above the mediocre concerns of a world that has lost sight of life after the storm.

Most people never see beyond their current circumstances. They rely on news forecasts and updates to tell them where their lives are headed. John Maxwell, one of the most influential speakers on success and leadership, once stated, "Change is inevitable. Growth is optional."

Life's storms will never cease to exist. Life will always ebb and flow, shift and change, but for you and me, there will always be a choice. I believe that some of the greatest casualties in life don't always come from the storms that we must confront, but from the narratives that we choose to consume. For you to be successful when confronted with a storm, your level of thinking needs to be at a higher altitude. Rise above the chaos, and learn how to discern the nature of the storm, and the season it has arrived in.

"Rise above the caos"

In all the time I've spent flying, I've learned that the guidelines for turbulence remain the same: Buckle up and remain seated. If your seatbelt is not secure, you risk injuring yourself and others. When life becomes turbulent, if your thinking is not secure, the same rules apply. You may wonder how to get to a higher altitude without flying. I am going to give you a few exercises that have helped me to elevate my thinking and get me through many of the storms in my life.

CHANGE YOUR ATMOSPHERE

There is an old saying, "If you're the smartest one in the room, you're in the wrong room." I believe successful people understand that the environment plays a fundamental role in growth and development.

Your desire to continue growing should supersede every other desire in your life. This is because growth is the essence of a vibrant life, full of success and abundant in possibility. You and I will never be perfect, but we can't allow our longing to develop to become subdued by complacency. This is the importance of surrounding yourself with people who have resolved within their minds that growth is not optional. These kinds of people have no issues with humility, which we will further discuss in another chapter. For now, I'll just say that they enjoy getting around different people and ideas.

Successful people understand we don't all look alike, and we don't all think the same. Most of the people who have mentored me taught me that there is an art in listening to people. We must have childlike curiosity and act as if every person we come in contact with knows a thing or two that we do not. Most of the time, this is true. But you must remain conscious of where you spend your time and who you spend it with.

I have heard many people say, "Show me your five closest friends, and I will accurately predict the next five years of your life." Your inner circle, friendships, and closest relationships – intimate and family – can make or break progress in your life. I have learned to expand my network to people who don't always think like me, don't look like me, don't talk like me, and probably have a very different upbringing than I did. This helps with the expansion of my perspectives.

When I can see things differently and with a deeper level of empathy, I can draw my own conclusions and ideas based on more than a superficial understanding of life. The boundaries that have played a role in the development of my beliefs can be expanded. Altogether, I am no longer interested in the person who can only offer me information attained by research or by cultural/religious bias. Put me in the room with the man or woman who has a passion for deeper understanding. Let me meet somebody who speaks from experience instead of just formal education. If you want to change your life, spend time with people who challenge every element of your thinking.

KNOW YOUR ALLIES AND YOUR ADVERSARIES

When you evaluate your life for expanding your thinking, it is a hard lesson to learn that the people you love are killing your progress. To attain your dreams, blind devotion is anything but bliss. Although it happens unintentionally, our desire to see the best in the people we love can stop us from seeing their true impact. When you aren't selective about who is in your corner and how they affect your thinking, you will accept beliefs that impede your ability to grow.

I don't endorse any and every success slogan that has been used to create interesting clichés. While I can appreciate out-of-the-box thinking, I have questioned what creates the box to begin with. How can you mingle perspectives with people who limit their experience to the source of their education? You and I will get a lot further in life with more allies and fewer adversaries.

For you to fully understand what I mean, I first need to define adversary in my intended use of the word. If you google the definition of the word, you will see it defined by Merriam Webster as "one who contends with, opposes, or resists: an enemy or opponent." The reality is that some relationships in your life stand in opposition to your ability to grow.

For some people, the groundbreaking period in their lives will require a ruthless effort to purge themselves of every person or thing that acts as an adversary to their aspirations. This is where having allies can be powerful. We can think of your allies as mentors, coaches, teachers, and people who share a mutual desire to see you grow and succeed. These people not only support you when you need it, but they will encourage you and often give you some reliable feedback. Those who understand where you are going and what you want to accomplish warrant constructive criticism. Beware of the people who read books and hear information, but who fail to act and implement.

Let's use formal education to illustrate the advantages of a group effort. Perhaps in school, you were assigned to a project with a group of people. For the sake of accomplishing that task, there was probably a need for you to put your heads together in order to bring it to completion. This old little idiom of "putting your heads together" is an instrumental approach in getting the assignment completed with efficacy. When you take time to think with other people, you may shorten your duration from point A to point B.

You'll hear wealthy people say the term "mastermind" often, and it refers to a bunch of successful people getting together and sharing ideas with each other. I've been to these, and they are think-tanks of more ideas and more ways to create impact and wealth. Fight to get around people who are smarter than you, sharper than you, and have more than you. That's how you learn. That's how you grow.

Whatever is deemed popular by the media or most of your friends won't be aligned with your goals or the vision you have of your future. To reject popular thinking means you'll need to be okay with feeling uncomfortable and having people around you thinking you're crazy. Forward thinkers are few and far between. Expansive thinking is a road less traveled.

We've already discussed how our thoughts become our realities. We must protect our thoughts by protecting those who impose on them. Revolution is not born from the societal standard of "Do as I say." Herd mentality requires very little effort, and it is, in fact, an adversary. To create the lives we desire, we must begin with the evolution of our thoughts.

WRITE IT DOWN

One night as I was winding down and getting ready for bed, I had a flood of different ideas regarding this book. I thought to myself that I would grab a pen and paper and write some of my thoughts down. It was really late, and my office was on the complete opposite side of my house. I didn't have any paper nearby, only a journal that had already been put to good use. I grabbed the closest pen next to my bedside table, and as I wrote down my thoughts, the pen broke, and black ink poured onto my hands. This incident admittedly looped me into thinking, "I can just write it in the morning, I am sure I will remember. I'm not about to get out of bed and walk around my house at 3:00 a.m. just to find a pen. By the time I get back, I probably won't remember, anyway."

At that moment, I took a glimpse of my bookshelf, where there was a yellow highlighter. I was slightly agitated, but I grabbed the highlighter and I scribbled down some words that would hardly make any sense in the morning. When I was done offloading my ideas, I made my way to the bathroom to wash the ink off my hands. I then made my way back to bed, and in no time I was examining the back of my eyelids.

In the morning, I revisited my scribbles from the night before. They were worth keeping. Every morning when I wake up and every night before I go to sleep, I sit and I reflect. I don't play on my phone; I don't check my texts and emails; I sit and I think in a calm state. This was a routine for me, and it was a habit I picked up from the successful people I have studied.

Journaling is a powerful way to get on top of your thoughts in order to view them objectively. People often tell you to think about what you are thinking about. Getting a journal and writing what comes to mind is a good way to do that. It allows you to get above your thoughts. It helps to detach some of the emotion that can keep you from reframing a particular thinking pattern that may be destructive.

You don't have to be a talented writer or have perfect penmanship to do this exercise. It is a simple and effective way for you to see what is happening in your mind. Keeping a journal nearby is a powerful way that you can get to know yourself. There are no rules or regulations, but I would encourage complete transparency. If you are anxious, then explain. If you have doubts, talk about why. Think of journaling as writing a letter to yourself. I have a friend who also uses a journal to write out their prayers, and they claim it can be a powerful way to go back and reflect on a spiritual relationship.

Thinking in a calm, deliberate state

See if you can carve out some time every day and night to sit, reflect, think. I have heard many personal testimonies from people who have used this exercise if they deal with anxiety or have a bad habit of procrastination.

If you take 15 minutes a day to write the first few things that come to mind, it helps to clear away some things that may stop you from taking action.

When I went back to check my journal entry from the previous night when my pen had burst, among the ideas for chapters and stories, I'd written the words, **"It's Already Done!"**

While this phrase has become personal to me in a lot of ways, it was not the original title of this book. In fact, I probably wrote it more out of habit than for any other reason at 3 a.m. When I read what I had written, I was contemplating various titles for the book. Although the title of this book isn't exactly, "It's Already Done," those words are included in the title.

Good thing I keep a journal.

.

THE MARVELOUS AND MIRACULOUS MIND

"Empowerment is that missing link that gets you from point A, hearing or reading good advice, to point B, actually applying it in a meaningful and sustainable way." – Dr. Caroline Leaf, communication pathologist and cognitive neuroscientist

When we suggest that a person is empowered, we are implying that they have cultivated the confidence to move toward their goals.

The depth of life for a successful man or woman is the measure of their perspective. Are they empowered or are they disempowered? Life through the eyes of those who have achieved their goals is merely a mirror image of what lies beneath the surface of human potential.

When you learn how to leverage your abilities, you become more resourceful, and it empowers you to move confidently toward your dreams. Your ability to produce results will come from the realization that your mind is a limitless tool — when it is not limiting you.

Early in 2011, I was speaking at a seminar in Charlotte, North Carolina. I can recall this day in my career as if it was yesterday. I was 21 years old at the time, making $400 a month. My bank account was hardly appealing, and my future felt like a dream that I'd never wake up from. At 24, I made my first $1 million. In three years my life was completely transformed. Since then I have had many stage appearances, but that day in North Carolina will remain a highlight in my life.

I walked off stage and headed to get some water. As I made my way to the water fountain, I was met by a man. He was unassuming and sincere, yet it felt as though our introduction was a divine orchestration of sorts. That man was Bob Proctor. He was very well respected in the personal growth industry, and known for his knowledge and expertise on the laws of success. While many people know him for his contributions to the teachings of these laws, and his role in the 2006 film, The Secret, I am lucky enough to call him my mentor.

"Bob Proctor – expert on the laws of success"

When we crossed paths that day in North Carolina, he began to ask me things that in my own free time, I had not considered. Things like, "How do you suppose you are up on that stage speaking?" and "What is it that you believe separates you from those who dream, but never make it beyond that point?"

Although his questions caught me off guard, I responded, not realizing at the time that my journey toward success was just beginning. I told him that I believed it was my hard work and dedication that landed me on that stage.

He was not convinced, and neither was I.

He continued, "What else?"

I told him that I had come from a wonderful family with two incredible parents. They made it their mission to raise me to be a man of discipline and integrity.

Still not satisfied with my answer, Proctor went on to explain that there were a lot of hardworking people with respectable families and a good upbringing. I had never thought about what it was that landed me on that stage. I was never taught to think about those things. Proctor knew something that I did not.

I determined then and there that I was an official student. Only this time, I was learning about the most important subject a man or woman can attempt to understand: themselves. From that moment forward, I decided that I would absorb the teachings and the lessons from a man who not only knew of abundance, but had it. A man who was in a state of overflow, willing and able to pour out that knowledge into my life.

The thing is, it doesn't matter how far along in your journey you are, there will always be someone ahead of you. Bob Proctor had set foot on his journey long before I had even discovered the path. As you read this chapter, and the chapters that follow, I want you to think of your mind as a sponge. I want you to absorb as much as possible, and then I want you to take this knowledge and allow it to saturate every area of your life.

Bob Proctor taught me many lessons about the mind, and how to nurture it in a way that inclines you to reach your goals. He saw something in me that I had not yet confronted. He invited me to Toronto, where for seven days we explored some of the more profound teachings of the mind. What he taught me in my time with him is what empowered me. It helped me to cultivate the confidence to do what I do. The entire purpose of this book is to impart that knowledge into your life, too.

WASH THE WINDOWS

Traveling the world has afforded me the luxury of becoming familiar with traditions and customs from religious backgrounds of all sorts. Although I was raised Jewish, I have an appreciation for some of the spectacular artistry found in Catholic cathedrals.

While traveling around Europe, I heard many stories about these notorious buildings and their stained glass windows. Once, when I was in Rome, I made it a priority to visit some of these. As I was quietly looking at the exquisite colors throughout one church, I overheard a woman speaking to some of the other tourists. I listened as she talked about the history behind some of the artistry, and I was amazed by what I heard.

There was a family with two children there. One of the children asked, "Mommy, how do they clean those windows?" The woman who was talking about the history looked at the young boy and replied with a smile, "The dirt and debris do not get washed off. They become a part of history."

For decades, artists have tried to replicate the exquisite detail. Some of the windows have been replicated with the dirt and all the tarnish in mind. The dirt is just as much a part of the window as the painted colors. This made me think. I believe that there are so many people who carry dirt and debris from their past, to the point that it becomes an identity. While we can call it beauty when we admire an architectural masterpiece, for you and me, the dirt becomes a belief system. Unlike the stained glass windows, however, your life becomes a mess instead of a masterpiece.

I have to wonder how many of you have been trying to get a clear vision of your future, while glaring through a tainted lens of your past. I believe for the majority of people reading this book, it's about time to start washing those windows.

PARADIGMS AND PROGRESS

In order to get a different perspective on life, you will need to change your paradigm. When I first heard the word paradigm, I didn't really understand it. I discovered that paradigms are a multitude of habits fixed in our subconscious mind. It's the programming from our parents, grandparents, teachers, professors, friends, family, and coaches. It's the stored-up crap that feeds and nourishes our thoughts.

Have you ever heard the saying, "March to the beat of your own drum?" Well, the majority of people are not successful in doing so because they are more accustomed to the symphonies of stupidity. Our focus, however, is not on the external world. My focus is to get you to understand the internal world, also referred to as the mind.

There are two parts of our mind—the conscious mind and the subconscious mind. We have the intellectual mind that allows us to choose, think, and imagine. This is your conscious mind. Then, we have our subconscious mind, where we must get emotionally involved with what we want. The subconscious mind triggers our body to take the actions necessary for us to achieve our goals and dreams. You may believe that you can make more money, get a promotion, start that business, etc. Yet every time you go to take action or make a decision, another voice says, "That's not happening!" Your subconscious weighs in with negativity.

I realized that, although we may think we can have whatever we want and really believe that, we are doing so only on a conscious level. In other words, how you feel about your life and what you are thinking about your life may not match up. There is an inconsistency somewhere in your mind that stops you from progressing every time you try to move forward.

The problem presents itself when we become stuck in a phase of our lives, and we don't know how we got there or why we can't seem to change. That is the power of a paradigm. This is what Bob Proctor helped me realize during the time he mentored me.

I want you to understand that "stuck" is an event. It happens to all of us at some point in time. As a species, mankind is in a constant state of evolution or growth. When you become stuck, it's an interruption in that pattern of growth. It becomes a program and a frequency of thought when you don't address it. It is the reason that addictions, when not positive, can destroy somebody's entire life.

My mission is to help you to see that the same thing that has driven you to the perils of stubborn cycles can also propel you to platforms of unbelievable progress. Before we move on, the other thing I want you to understand is this — to stay stuck is a decision that you are making daily. *Stuck is an occurrence, stay is an option.* If you are looking around at your life right now, wondering how it is you got to where you are, look no further because I have just told you. If you find that in five, ten, fifteen, twenty years that you are in that same place, it's likely because you read this book, but you didn't absorb anything that was said.

If you return to this chapter, with no change in your life, it's because you have overstayed your welcome in a particular 'season.' It's time to move on. It's time to make a decision to change. You do this by shifting your paradigm. The two ways to shift your paradigm are through an emotional impact AND through constant, spaced-repetition of the right information.

IF IT WEIGHS ON YOUR CONSCIENCE

The average man or woman never makes a sufficient amount of progress in their lives. Therefore, the longings of their spiritual nature go unsatisfied and unfulfilled.

One of the most empowering truths is that we have the ability to revolt against mundane/ average forms of life. In fact, we were created to do so. You were designed with an insatiable hunger to seek your potential and fulfill your purpose. You and I will never be satisfied with the way things are, no matter how much we try to fool ourselves. The spirit within you will never receive anything less than the person God intended you to be.

It is entirely possible to have a life and yet not be alive. We will discuss this further later on, but for now I want to explore how you change subconscious programming. I want to talk about emotional impact. Les Brown once shared a powerful statement formerly stated by a close friend of his, Dr. Myles Munroe. Brown said, *"The graveyard is the richest place on earth, because it is here that you will find all the hopes and dreams that were never fulfilled, the books that were never written, the songs that were never sung, the inventions that were never shared, and the cures that were never discovered."*

I don't know about you, but I think that if we look at the state of our society, we can't afford to store our treasures in earthly places any longer. While I am fully aware that the former context of that statement had nothing to do with the cemetery, and my intention is not to dishonor the original author, one of the greater tragedies of life is that people often bury their dreams instead of living them. When we fail to acknowledge the potential within us, we are haunted ruthlessly by the should haves and could haves of our decisions.

Science and religion point to the idea that we, as human beings, can build our reality through our thoughts, our feelings, our emotions, and our actions. One of the things that perplexes me about humanity is that we have a unique ability to leverage our emotions, but that is a role that has been reversed. Most of the time, our emotions leverage us. Our emotions or our feelings are unbelievably powerful. They guide us, they signal to us, and they move us from place to place along our journey.

It is rare for an emotional impact to shift your paradigm. These moments in life are few and far between. It is the devastating impact of an event, a crisis or a loss that occurs. It can also be the miracle moments when a child is born or you fall in love for the first time. These emotional occurrences are so deeply connected to your spirit that they create a paradigm shift. They become a part of who you are. They are so immensely impactful in your conscious state of awareness that they connect directly with your subconscious, communicating a directional shift in your life. They signal to your subconscious mind, "This is important! Pay attention!" In these moments of immense emotional stimulation, your normal pattern is interrupted. Your life has manifested before you. You have the perfect opportunity to change. You and I can't rely on an emotional impact to change our paradigm. It would become a tiring process and very few people would ever be successful.

REAP WHAT YOU REPEAT

Zig Ziglar said, *"Repetition is the mother of learning, the father of action, which makes it the architect of accomplishment."*

When I was younger, I remember watching people like Michael Jordan play basketball. I would watch Mike Tyson knock people out. When I got a little older, I started looking up to entrepreneurs like Mark Cuban and Grant Cardone. As I started studying personal growth, I greatly admired people like Tony Robbins, Jim Rohn, Earl Nightingale, and, of course, my mentor, Bob Proctor. I can remember my constant mental questions: "I wonder if I could be that athletic. Can I be as great as them? Can I accomplish as many things as they've accomplished? Can I earn this type of money? Could I own a private jet one day? Can I speak on stage in front of tens of thousands of people and create a real impact in their lives?"

I can bet that you have the same or similar questions in your mind. I'm not talking about comparison. That is of a completely different nature. I am talking about that innate nudge within your spirit that inclines you to seek greatness. Comparison suppresses that voice. Curiosity is of a divine influence that pushes you to discover the fundamental things that make you brilliant.

We are all spiritual beings living in a physical body, and we all have higher faculties. Here is something that can serve you in the long run: The voice that compares and criticizes, and the voice that drives your curiosity sound almost the same. They both belong to you. One had been programmed, and the other was God's gift to you. The difference is that one speaks from doubt and the other from faith. The key is to identify which one has made its way into the primary paradigm by which you act, think, and choose. Which one are you listening to? My guess would be that for the majority of people, it would be the one that suppresses you and holds you back. That is the one that has been on constant repetition throughout your day.

I would like you to suppress the suppressor, and turn up the voice that calls you to step into your true potential. I did it! It took some work, but the voice I hear is that which empowers me.

We like to think that we are so different from the people who have made it to where they are. We do this because it gives us an excuse to opt out of doing the work. What you are really doing is trying to let yourself off the hook. You are God's highest form of creation, capable of anything and everything. The quicker you realize and accept this, the quicker you will move into a place of power and prosperity.

"No accidents – everything in this universe happens by law"

As I dive into the six spiritual faculties in the chapters to follow, I want you to understand that everything in this universe happens by law — there are no accidents. Wealth, abundance, fortunes, and happiness are not limited to luck or circumstance. They are the evidence that you summed up by the compounding decisions you make daily.

As you read on, I am going to teach you about mental faculties. These six faculties are:

will,
reason,
imagination,
intuition,
memory, and
perception.

Understanding these six faculties and studying them over and over will help you to shift your paradigm. It did for me in 2011, and I promise that the same can be done by and for you, too.

When you lay your head down tonight, I want you to constantly tell yourself, "It's Already Done!"

Be assured, it certainly is!

Part II

A NEW WAY OF THINKING

This portion of the book is dedicated to you.

Although I do not know you as intimately as I do myself, my wife, my friends, or anybody in my family, I know that you are capable of accomplishing extraordinary things!

This world has conditioned us throughout our lives to live through our five basic senses. Those senses include your ability to see, taste, smell, touch, and hear. Apart from your experience of the world within the boundaries of those five senses, there are greater depths and levels to be encountered and explored.

"School diploma is different than Diploma of Life of Success"

The average person's progress is not sufficient enough to satisfy the spiritual need to grow. It is not enough to aid in the development of a legacy that outlasts lucrative careers or momentary phases of being "well-known" for your accolades. Your life legacy can be thought of as your contributions to this world. It could be the contributions you make to the people you love and the generations that are coming after you. Exploring the deeper levels that attribute to the attainment of success leads you to discover the infinite levels of human potential. This is where you encounter your God-given abilities. These are the faculties of your mind, which make up who you are and what you are capable of. The discovery of these faculties allows you to embody the infinite potential of such a simple affirmation as, **"It's Already Done!"**

The journey can feel daunting and unattainable at times. Rarely, if ever, should you rely on your feelings! Remember, the primary goal of your mind is to keep you safe. Success hardly feels safe. It involves risk, discipline, and, most importantly, desire. You must constantly strive to move forward, beyond your supposed limitations.

In this section of the book, my chief aim is to reveal to you why and how it's possible to move forward, beyond your supposed limitations.

We will talk about the different levels of learning, comprehension, and execution. I will also touch on more of the laws that govern our universe. I will ask a series of questions with a goal to help you discover the role that you play in this marvelous thing we call life. I want to make myself extremely clear: I can tell you what desire is, and I can do my best to illustrate the power of desire. Nobody, including myself, can give you desire. What I mean by that is simply this: if you don't want to put in the work, learn this information with every intention to implement it, and if you don't have any inclination whatsoever to succeed in life, I can't help you.

I don't believe there is a single book or formula that can do the work for you, or create what we know as desire. The power of this knowledge is something I believe in, but the amount of progress you make is entirely up to you. I am excited to share this knowledge with you because I believe it's a gift that comes from the creator of our universe — the gift people are afraid of because they don't understand it, the gift that sheds light within a world that tries to keep most things hidden in the shadows of obscurity.

I dedicate this portion of the book to the men and women who have grown impatient with mediocrity. These are the kinds of people who are unamused by the social media facades.

They are unwilling to settle for anything less than their ultimate best.

I meet these kinds of people every time I reach a new level of success, and I have to wonder, will I meet you one day?

Will you let your story be one that helps make your world a little bigger and brighter?

Many people won't settle for complacency. Are you one of them?

You know my story. Are you ready to write, discover, or rediscover yours?

LET'S GO!!

THE FOUNDATION OF ACHIEVEMENT

*"Beware of ignorance when in motion; look out for inexperience when
in action and beware of the majority when mentally poisoned with
misinformation, for collective ignorance does not become wisdom."*
— *William J. H. Boetcker*

I have trouble wrapping my mind around formal education. I can
understand the reasons our society praises modern-day school institutions.
But I can hardly agree with the current varieties of curriculum being
taught to younger generations. This is merely my personal opinion. Yet I
make my case with sincerity and conviction when I politely dismiss the
arguments regarding the usefulness of curriculum as they pertain to the
topic of success.

For the average American, there is a required 12 years of formal
education. As you gradually make your way up to more advanced levels
of learning, your success in school comes down to the grades on your
report card, all combined together as your GPA (Grade Point Average).
You are then accepted into different colleges based on that GPA. Getting
straight A's is the typical standard for academic intelligence, but the reality
at hand is pretty dismal when it comes to the real world. My objective
is not to bash the systems and institutions. I agree that they serve their
purpose. I do, however, believe that the lessons taught in school are not the
lessons that will have you on your way to financial freedom, or any kind of
freedom at all.

None of this is meant to discourage you. In fact, I was 24 years old
when I discovered the concepts in this chapter. I had no idea that there
were different levels in learning, none of which are mentioned in the
textbooks. I believe that our best lessons are learned through experience,
but what is experience without awareness? When you gain a greater
awareness about life, how do you move into accountability, or acceptance?
Beyond the acceptance phase, where you have realized you are responsible
for your success, what are the actions and alterations that need to be made?

Here is a formula, just one token of wisdom that I received from Bob Proctor. When I really started to understand the concept behind this formula, it granted me the realization that straight A's expand far beyond the scope of your report card. The real A's to be emphasized are the ones applicable to living a successful life. This simple formula is known as "The Three A's: Awareness, Acceptance, and Alteration." This formula helps us begin to learn other concepts of success. It brings us to topics such as the four levels of learning, the different laws of the universe, and, of course, the different faculties of our mind. In this chapter, you will learn about the four levels of learning, as well as the three A's. These will serve as the foundation of your achievement.

PHASE ONE: IGNORANCE IS NOT BLISS

At dinner with a good friend of mine, he shared a comical experience he had on returning home for Thanksgiving. His family had invited their new neighbors to dinner. My friend grew up in Tennessee. If you have ever heard of southern hospitality, you wouldn't be surprised by the invitation.

These neighbors had a six-year-old son and a five-year-old daughter who loved to be the center of attention. When it was time to eat, the kids were arguing back and forth. In an attempt to interrupt their commotion, the mom asked her son to say the blessing over their meal. With absolutely no hesitation, he bowed his head, grabbed his family members hands and began singing happy birthday to the Lord, followed by a loud AMEN. This was unconscious incompetence at its finest.

It is, *"When the individual does not understand or know how to do something and does not recognize the deficiencies or where they are going wrong, they may deny the usefulness of the skill. The individual must recognize their own incompetence, and the value of the new skill, before moving on to the next stage."*

"Unconscious incompetence"

In short, it's the complete opposite of the modern slang often seen on social media posts, abbreviated IYKYK, which translates to, "If you know, you know." *Unconscious incompetence means you don't know what you don't know.*

For you to be successful, you must be aware of the four levels of learning and know which level you are operating from. This is part of Awareness.

In my early 20s, I knew that if I wanted a change in my life, I would have to start with myself. The difference between those who will do what is necessary versus those who will live life as the victim of circumstance is this: Successful people understand ignorance is the farthest thing from bliss. If you look at the word ignorance, you will see part of the word **"ignore,"** which comes from the Latin word **"ignoranti**a," meaning a "lack of wisdom or knowledge; not knowing."

Ignorance plagues our world today, and I believe that ignorance is one of the greatest threats to self-awareness and success. When you choose to ignore the truth about who you are and what you are capable of, you will suffer the consequences that come from a life of "knowing" what is wrong with everyone else and everything else and "not knowing" (ignoratia) yourself. Have you ever stopped to consider what's getting you to the current results in your life? What inhibits you from achieving a different result?

By now, you are probably aware that your results are produced from the actions you have been taking. Your actions are the descendants of your thinking patterns and the paradigms within your subconscious mind. I hope you understand that. Unconscious Incompetence would probably be your primary level of learning if you have not grasped these things after making it this far into the book. I have a little bit more faith in you than to believe you are on this level. At some point, however, we all are on the level of unconscious incompetence. When you are at this level, there is hardly much thought involved.

When I was in kindergarten, I didn't know I was being programmed by my environment to follow orders, directions, and be conditioned to be a slave to a paycheck for the rest of my life. It's quite sad, isn't it? We take kids who can barely walk and begin to program them to be a drone in the assembly line their entire lives. Look, I'm not sitting here talking down on jobs, I'm just very up on opportunity and individuals controlling their own destiny. I believe everyone should control their own time and money. It's understandable for a child to be unconscious incompetent for their first few years of living, but it's not okay to be that way in your 30s and 40s, and even beyond.

The sad truth is that many of the people around us are unconsciously incompetent. What's worse is that they actually believe they understand how to become successful. The problem is that we go to school for so many years and are never taught the fundamentals of success and achievement. I believe that this is done on purpose, to keep people enslaved in the prison of financial hardship. The worst part about financial prisons, mental prisons, and any other kind of box that you find identity in, is that there are no visible boundaries. The only way out is through your awareness turned into acceptance, followed by making changes.

PHASE TWO: AT THE CROSSROADS

The next level is conscious incompetence. At this point of learning, you have become aware of the fact that you may not have all the answers, solutions, or perfected techniques.

This is the portion of learning where people are more likely to give up. A good example is strength training at the gym. If you are an athlete, you can likely relate to the frustration of this phase. It's that point in time where you've been snacking on too many Oreos with peanut butter or your nightly ice cream treat, and you decide you are going to work it off in the gym. If you haven't been consistent at the gym until this point, you might realize that you can't lift as much weight as you thought. Perhaps your technique is subpar due to a loss of muscle. It can be disheartening, and when you don't have a clear goal in mind, it can be defeating.

Another good example is golf. I don't speak on behalf of the professional golfers. I don't play golf, but I've heard many stories. Golf, to my understanding, is not much of a reactive sport, which makes it more of a mental game. I have friends who play as a hobby, and sometimes they will even incentivize each other by throwing in some money for the guy who has the best game. Some of my friends, when they're about to tee off, envision they're Tiger Woods and end up looking like Happy Gilmore when they make their swing. They are aware that they should practice before they putt. At this level of learning, it's wise to begin setting realistic expectations without forfeiting your standards. With conscious incompetence, *"Though the individual does not understand or know how to do something, he or she does recognize the deficit, as well as the value of developing a new skill to address the deficit. The making of mistakes can be integral to the learning process at this stage."*

At that moment in time, you have to know you're deficient, and now you need to decide to change that. Acceptance is vital at this point because it will land you at the crossroads where you decide to: A) make the necessary changes and adjustments, or B) give up and walk away from your goals. At this point, you get to determine whether you will remain incompetent or become invincible.

"Making mistakes can be integral to the learning process"

When I was in the third grade, my family home was in Columbus, Ohio. I can remember vividly one night making my way down to our basement. I was notorious for exploring, and I had a very active imagination. My curiosity, in fact, has led me to where I am today. Back then, as I made my way down to our basement one night (probably putting off my homework), I stumbled across some old books. My parents had a collection stashed on an old wooden shelf beside the water pumps and heating system. As I ventured over to the shelf and began to wipe the dust off, I could make out the title of the books, but I had no clue what they were about. The books were: *Awaken the Giant Within*, *The Magic of Believing*, *Think and Grow Rich*, and *How to Win Friends and Influence People*, along with several others. Alongside the books, I found an entire collection of audio tapes, labeled "Tony Robbins."

While I had very little understanding concerning the information they contained, it was like I had hit a jackpot and found my buried treasure. I grabbed some of the books, along with the tapes, and I brought them up to my room. In school, I was learning about the multiplication tables, and at the gym how to hit a baseball. When I arrived home from school, I would visit my little basement stash. When I got a bit older, I began to realize that the stuff written in these books was nothing like what we were learning in the textbooks. No one was talking about goal-setting or developing a burning desire.

Eventually, I started to listen to the tapes where the word "success" was mentioned constantly. While my comprehension of the information was not much developed, I can remember feeling like Superman when I started to really listen. Fast forward to 2016 and then again to 2018, success was in the playbook — I knew of it, I heard of it, but I was at the crossroads. I accepted that for me to have the kind of success that was written in those books and recorded on those tapes, the journey would require more on my part. I had to go all in.

PHASE THREE: OFF TO THE RACES!

The third phase of learning is conscious competence. I look at this phase as the turning point of your young adult life, where you finally obtain your driver's license. It's your first time getting behind the wheel without mom and dad there to coach you or yell at you. At this point, you have earned the right to operate some powerful machinery. But this new level of freedom also comes with a new level of responsibility. When you first learned to drive, if you weren't a rebel, you likely went the extra mile to make sure everything was good to go. You knew what to do: buckle up, adjust your mirrors, adjust the seat, maybe pick a song before you shift into gear. You paid extra attention to this new responsibility, and the moment you shifted into drive, there was a certain level of concentration that was probably very apparent.

This is conscious competence.

It's the phase where, *"The individual understands or knows how to do something. However, demonstrating the skill or knowledge requires concentration. It may be broken down into steps, and there is heavy conscious involvement in executing the new skill."*

"*Showing conscious competence*"

Perhaps now it's okay to post a picture to social media of your brand new car, captioned "IYKYK!" It's the point in time where you are consciously aware of what to do and how to do it. Although you've become aware of your new level of expertise, it will still take a dedicated effort to continue learning. It's the phase of learning where repetition becomes extraordinarily powerful. Concentration is a necessary component in successful execution. It's where practice begins to pay off. You've made it to a state of progression, and the feelings are exhilarating.

Conscious competence requires many hours of studying the right material. This is one of my personal favorite stages of learning. In this stage, you can also begin to cultivate a passion and hunger for your goals. It's primetime to maximize as much as you can on building that momentum by fueling that hunger. Read the books, watch the podcasts, listen to the tapes, and tell people. I've been inspired by Mary Oliver, an American poet who won the National Book Award and the Pulitzer Prize, who was born in Maple Heights, Ohio, a little over two hours away from where I grew up in Bexley. She wrote, "*Pay Attention. Be Astonished. Tell people about it.*"

There is a lot of power in excitement. The flipside is that it takes a lot of courage to begin to share that excitement with others, because opposition and criticism are inevitable. Never let this stop you.

When you're consciously competent, you have the ability to execute at a high-level, but you must constantly remind yourself how and what you need to do to produce the results you desire. Sharing your joy with others won't always come with reciprocation.

Keep doing it. The journey toward mastery is like practicing a field sport. When you look to the stands, nobody will be cheering you on. It is only once you are off to the races that people begin to get loud. Keep running your race. Success is not about your spectators. Success is not about stadiums and it's not about status. Success is about the stride, the moment of decision to keep moving forward.

As I close out this segment about learning, I am going to leave you with two quotes from Malcolm Gladwell's 2008 book, Outliers: The Story of Success: "Success is a function of persistence and doggedness and the willingness to work hard for twenty-two minutes to make sense of something that most people would give up on after thirty seconds." You may have heard the gist of the second quote from achievement experts. Gladwell writes, *"In fact, researchers have settled on what they believe is the magic number for true expertise: ten thousand hours."*

PHASE FOUR: GO WITH THE FLOW

The last phase of learning is known as unconscious incompetence.

Simply put, it is the point in time where a person has hit the level of mastery. Charles Duhigg in his book, *The Power of Habit: Why We Do What We Do in Life and Business,* wrote, *"Champions don't do extraordinary things. They do ordinary things, but they do them without thinking, too fast for the other team to react. They follow the habits they've learned."* It's the point in time where all the practice has become the sum total of an innate performance. You don't have to think about how to do something because it is second nature.

Unconsciously competent is a state of being. I call this state the Flow State.

At this level, you are creating, manifesting, and taking the correct actions necessary to achieve your goals. "The individual has had so much practice with a skill that it has become "second nature" and can be performed easily. As a result, the skill can be performed while executing another task." In 2012, when I earned my first six figures in business, I got into the Flow State. I was attracting the situations, opportunities, and people I needed to take my business and life to the next level. In fact, I had been doing this for such an extended period of time that I came to a place where I could deliver this teaching to others.

I was in a position to coach others because I had become a master of my craft. Unconscious competence is where excellence meets elegance. It's where all of the effort put forth begins to work in harmony with the laws of the universe. Make no mistake, this phase would not exist if not for extreme focus and relentless pursuit. It does not manifest without the A's of Awareness, cAceptance, and Alteration. It harnesses the power of each of these, and shifts into the foundation of your achievement. You learned to eliminate both internal and external distractions. The intention has been set on the attainment of your goals. Moment by moment, you begin to mold your life to receive the fullness of your silent prayers. It's at this fourth phase of learning that you've come to the progressive realization of an affirmed belief that suggests it's already done!

FOLLOW THROUGH AND STAY DISCIPLINED

"We are all the same. Some are male, some are female, but outside of the reproductive system,
we are all the same. You might think of age, race, and cultural differences.
The only difference there is in appearance, and the truth is rarely in the appearance of things.
Throw us all into a hot fire, and we are all reduced to the same level.
Use your higher faculties. Look within." – Bob Proctor

I often wonder how different life would be if those who paved the way for success, impact, courage, and unity had decided that they would give up on their dreams because they didn't feel like showing up. I think about how different this world would be if the successful few had allowed age or ethnicity to dictate what they could and could not accomplish.

On August 28th, 1963, Martin Luther King Jr. gave his iconic speech, "I Have a Dream," at a civil rights rally in Washington, D.C. He was 34 years old. At 76 years old, Nelson Mandela became the first black president of South Africa. In 1957, at 53 years old, Dr. Seuss became a pioneer in children's literature with the release of *The Cat in the Hat* and *How the Grinch Stole Christmas!* Anne Frank was only 12 years old when she wrote the *Diary of Anne Frank*, published in 1947 in Amsterdam and then in the following years in over 70 languages. Her work later became one of the most widely read accounts of the Holocaust. My main point here is that age is not an excuse.

I was in my early 20s when I got obsessed with the idea of success. That passion led me to study the people who had achieved extraordinary things. At the time, I was just a college kid, eating Taco Bell every other night, drinking, partying, and messing around. I was far from where I am today, but I had conviction. I knew who I wanted to be and where I wanted to be, and going from a dorm room to my parents' spare bedroom after graduation would not cut it. Conviction, however, would not change the direction my life was heading. I quickly discovered that conviction was useless without action, and those actions would also be useless without consistency.

Within me was a desire to know the magic formula. I wanted to understand the mentalities of those I admired. I wanted to learn about the habits of the world's greatest thought leaders, game changers, and money makers. I studied people and I studied successful relationships.

I learned that the quality of your life doesn't equate to the wealth you acquire, but instead the depth of impact you have on others. I quickly found out that extraordinary people aren't people who have superpowers that made them better than everyone else. Instead, they mastered the art of doing the small things daily. They mastered discipline, and they stuck to their course of action, unfazed by the detours and distractions life had thrown in front of them.

By the grace of God and a lot of those same daily disciplines that make every day people rise above the rest, I was fortunate enough to meet some of the brilliant minds and people I had decided to model. One of these people was Grant Cardone, a real estate legend who has amassed $1.5 billion and probably well over that by now in his business ventures. I also met some other great entrepreneurs such as John Paul DeJoria, best known as the co-founder of Paul Mitchell hair products, and the Patrón Spirits Company.

The circle of people I surrounded myself with continued to shape my growth and my level of knowledge in different spaces, helping me to create and learn the habits of those who had achieved exactly what I was going after.

I was willing to do whatever it took to breathe in success, and to surround myself with people who don't just "talk the talk." They live and breathe success every single day, creating generational wealth for their families. I remained humble and willing to listen and learn from several specialists in their fields. I didn't allow my pride to get the better of me when it came to being a student of success.

I committed to my development, which later led me to more and more opportunities to meet and speak with people who had what I wanted.

While these people had accumulated the megawealth and the economic status that I had wanted to achieve, money did not drive my desire to get in front of these people. Instead, I developed an insatiable hunger for more, more of everything that encompasses a successful life: more moments, more joy, more depth in my relationships, more passion, more fulfillment, and more love for life. Getting more money was the byproduct of all the hard work and discipline it took for me to manifest more in my life.

"Don't aspire to make a living – aspire to make a difference"

Denzel Washington, one of my favorite actors and highly celebrated for his film and stage work, said, *"Don't aspire to make a living, aspire to make a difference."*

Although money has a way of drawing people in, I can promise you it doesn't guarantee your joy. When I got close to the right people and studied their methods and patterns, I noticed several things that were synonymous with success. These people didn't wake up one day with the abundance of fortune, health, and happiness they had envisioned at a young age. There was no overnight success or get-rich-quick formula they followed. Not even one of these people lived with the notion that money would be their ticket to happiness. In fact, it was quite the opposite.

Influential people all understand that happiness is the ticket to more money, more health, more of everything that you and I could imagine.

Happiness is one of the key disciplinary ingredients needed to create those outcomes.

In my decade of studying success and studying the people who I knew were successful, I realized that truth. Before I could occupy the success space, I had to observe it.

As I write this book, I want to pause for a serious discussion with you. I want you to consider that you are offered two different outcomes, and you can choose only one or the other. Pretend that a genie comes to you, not Will Smith, but an actual mystical genie shows up in your dream one night. This genie says to you, "When you wake up in the morning, I will grant you one outcome of your choosing. Tomorrow morning I will give you a life of riches and fortune or, if you so choose, your life can be full of joy and an abundance of happiness. The choice is yours — do you want to be rich, or do you want to be happy?"

Research has shown that nine out of ten times, the average person would pick happiness. But if the genie came to you and offered another alternative, phrased slightly differently and you were presented with the choice of, "I can grant you the ability to be a better person, constantly growing and progressing, or I can just make you rich," it is assumed that you would probably choose to be rich. Interesting, isn't it? The fundamental difference in choices has nothing to do with the answer you give. The answer you give nine out of ten times comes from the amount of effort required of you.

In short, most people are not willing to put in the extra work. In real life, there is no magic genie.

In real life, your achievements will always be the sum of your beliefs + your attitude + the actions that you take. It was this formula that I had discovered to be the most common active attribute among the people I had studied.

Unsurprisingly, I learned that the difference between an average person and the people who apply this formula to their lives is that average people would choose instant gratification over having to put in the time and the effort to achieve big things in their life. Growth and development require discipline and hard work. Your daily decisions about what you are going to do moment by moment will determine whether you ever experience the life of your dreams. Or, as Les Brown stated, whether you add to the wealth found within a graveyard. Once I understood that my destiny came down to the compounded effect of my beliefs, my attitude, and my daily decisions, my life changed.

FIVE PLUS SIX WILL DO THE TRICK

We must make our best effort to learn from history, and I am not talking about the curriculum in the textbooks used in schools. I am talking about the people who have made history, the people that you and I were not taught about in school. We must look at the lesson plans they lived by.

Although people often experience their lives via the tangible manifestations of a physical experience, there is another side that we do not perceive. It is more powerful than the physical. We are all spiritual beings having a physical experience. Sure, some of us have different formal educational levels, and we all have different quirks that make up our character. But we have many things in common. Many of those things are positive, but it is likely that you have been groomed and taught to focus on the negative, destructive ones. The result leads to unfruitful lives where we reap only the ailments of the toxic patterns and paradigms of the people that surround us.

I believe the Torah and other good books warn against such manipulation, teaching us not to succumb to the patterns and programming of this world. If you ever wish to follow through with your dreams and tap into your higher faculties, you must study. Study yourself and study the successful people that have gone before you.

Have you ever heard people say history repeats itself? I always found that to be interesting. I believe history repeats itself because people willfully ignore the lessons of the past. They allow fear to dictate their focus, and thus faith almost becomes obsolete. How can you avoid a pattern you have been programmed to pay attention to, since childhood?

There are patterns that make people successful and there are also patterns that make people perpetually broke, busted, and disgusted. Ever since man and woman first set foot on Earth, we have been gifted with senses that allow us to experience life. The five senses we are conditioned to believe are the maximum capabilities within humanity are the abilities to hear, see, smell, taste, and touch. Right? Wrong. You learned about your five senses. Great! Now let me teach you about your six faculties, something that I learned from Bob Proctor. He often said, *"if you change your perception, you will eliminate the problem."*

"If you change your perception, you will eliminate the problem."

You are probably wondering how this has anything to do with following through and staying disciplined, but, in fact, it has everything to do with what we have covered so far. If you can learn how to live your life beyond the realm of a physical experience created by your five senses and you can discipline your mind to decide, and to continue to decide, it is in those disciplined moments that you tap into the spiritual awareness that transforms your life. It was the fundamental knowledge of these spiritual faculties that took from me $0 to over $30 million by the age of 30 years old, and now much more. Never use age as an excuse!

If you want to increase your income and become financially free, you must become disciplined. You must discipline your senses to work for you, instead of being controlled by them. You must discipline your hearing so that you understand the language of money. You must discipline your sense of sight so that you see only what pulls you toward your vision. You must discipline your sense of smell and taste so that food and unhealthy eating habits do not control you. Be disciplined about your lifestyle choices. Go exercise, move your body DAILY!

Finally, discipline your touch, get around the things that you want, go, and sit in the car that you wish to drive, place yourself in front of the things you would like to have, try on the clothes you want to wear, go into the furniture stores you dream about. Jim Rohn has said, *"The backbone to every eager desire is discipline."* Discipline your five senses daily, consistently, without contemplation of skimping out. If you don't have all five, then use the ones you have! Most people think they must "work" for money, and that's just not true. We work for satisfaction. We provide value to earn money. There's a major difference.

THE MOST SUCCESSFUL GAME

*"I hated every minute of training, but I said,
'Don't quit. Suffer now and live the rest of your life as a champion.'" –
Muhammad Ali*

When I was growing up, I would spend my free time pretending to be some of my childhood heroes. Whether it was Kobe Bryant or Michael Jordan, the driveway was my stadium, and winning was mine to choose.

As I dribbled the ball up and down the court (my driveway), I could hear the crowd yelling intensely as I handled the ball. With seconds left in the game, it was up to me to sink the game-winning buzzer-beater. In my mind, it was all real. Those winning driveway moments were cultivating the drive and the discipline that landed me where I am today.

I remember running into the house for dinner, my hands black from the pavement and my entire body covered in sweat. It is crazy to think back to the days I was a child when nothing was impossible, and I could create scenarios in my mind that were as real as the live event itself. My driveway went from a sold-out NBA arena to a stadium at Wimbledon. I would spend hours outside, hitting the tennis ball against the garage until the day grew dark. Starting at a young age, I was captivated by the winner's mentality, and I wanted to be the best at anything and everything I had set out to do. Eventually, I got pretty good at playing tennis, but it was my younger sister Maddie who went on to earn a scholarship to play at a college level in Southern California. Shout out to my little sister, Maddie — she is amazing!

In seventh grade, I decided that I wanted to try out for the different teams that represented my middle school in Bexley, OH. I tried out for the basketball team, the tennis team, and the football team. The hours that I spent playing in my driveway had paid off, and at the time I quickly advanced to a position as the power forward on the basketball team in my seventh- and eighth-grade years. In high school, I focused on football and tennis. There was something about the game and even most of the practices that compelled me to keep pushing and keep training myself to get better and better. Sports gave me something to look forward to. It was an outlet for me, and it was probably one of the few things about school that I thoroughly enjoyed. Sports taught me about leadership, discipline, tenacity, grit, and perseverance. It taught me patience and the importance of accountability.

Measuring 5'9" and weighing 185 pounds my senior year of high school, I earned my position as a co-captain of the football team. While I was proud at that moment for all the hard work that I had put in and the memories I had accumulated, I realized that I couldn't exactly jump out of the gym or run a 4.4 40-yard dash.

Once I realized I was not going to become a professional athlete, I took all that drive, determination, and competitive spirit I had built up in mysel and fueled it all into business. I remember saying, "Man, I don't need to dunk a basketball or score a touchdown to become a millionaire in business — this is my thing: I am going to excel in the business world! I'm going to take over the world of business!" Sure, I would reminisce about the hot summer workouts that would have me and my teammates puking, and about the wins, the losses, and the friendships I had built with the other guys on my team. I was grateful for all the discipline and lessons that playing sports had taught me, but I retired my cleats with the understanding that I would show up to the next chapter of my life a better character and a better player because of it.

I have found time and time again that most people don't reach their highest potential, not because they are unable, but because they are unwilling to work hard for it.

In 1978, a sophomore at Laney High School in Wilmington, North Carolina, known to his friends as "Mike," tried out for the school basketball team. Mike was cut from the varsity team because they considered him too short at 5'9". The following year, after leading the JV team in several 40-point games, with hard work as well as a big growth spurt, Mike went on to play at a varsity level where he eventually led his team to a No. 1 State ranking. Most of you probably know of the man in this story, drafted by the Chicago Bulls in 1984, winning 6 championships in a row. We still know Michael Jordan today as one of the best players of all time. He was willing to do whatever it took to win, and his philosophy and determination on the court landed him in the Hall of Fame and continues to carry him through his life now.

> *"Be true to the game, because the game will be true to you.*
> *If you try to shortcut the game, then the game will shortcut you.*
> *If you put forth the effort, good things will be bestowed upon you.*
> *That's truly about the game, and in some ways, that's about life, too."*
>
> *– Michael Jordan*

Some of the world's greatest athletes have taught us some valuable lessons about life and success. Babe Ruth, another sporting hero, known for the tremendous number of home runs he had hit in baseball, also led the league in the number of strikeouts which, according to the "experts" of his time, was a disgrace. None of that mattered, though, because today he is known most for his accomplishments. His lesson: "Never let the fear of striking out keep you from stepping up to bat."

There are few things more exciting than watching your favorite team take the game-winning title in a championship game. I guess the more profound thing to consider is the fact that the average person is willing to spend 700 dollars on a ticket to watch their favorite teams play. And the same thing could not be said when it comes to investing, saving, or applying that same amount of money to a dream of their own. Most people are willing to be spectators of someone else's dream rather than a player in their own life.

FROM BALLER TO BUSINESS

From a young age, I had a natural curiosity about the world of business (remember that stash of books I found in the basement of my childhood home). I was fortunate to grow up in a household where both of my parents worked hard and instilled a passion for achievement in my core values. Both of my parents were highly invested in the insurance industry, and my dad had accumulated a wealth of knowledge in the space using the same books and audios that one would purchase to level up their expertise.

One day, my dad handed me a book that many of you have read or been advised to read by people in the realm of business, marketing, and personal growth. The book was Rich Dad, Poor Dad, by Robert Kiyosaki. This book taught me the foundational principles that I live by to this day. I can remember being profoundly affected by the wisdom the book imparted. I took it a step further and printed in big letters on the inside of my biology book, "Think big and kick ass." My teacher at the time was not thrilled about the tactics I had shared and dismissed me from class. Business was my blueprint, and almost immediately I applied the methods and ideas of business to my habits and behaviors.

I knew that in order to get to the top, I would have to come up with a unique edge that others before me had not executed, and I had to further build upon the definition of that edge by adding value to myself and others.

I leveraged the disciplines and tactics I had gained playing sports in the previous years, which led me to discover what other skilled players in the industry have identified as the sport of business. They centered on the ideas that had revolutionized this space around gaining an edge over your competition and everyone else in your field. The end goal was like that of elite athletes, do everything you can to stack the odds in your favor and make winning your principal aim. Reading this book, and others like it, is a good way to recognize the habits within your own life that will contribute to developing that edge. The reason you read, the reason you write out your goals and you prioritize time with intention is one of the stepping stones to greatness. It is a step toward creating your own unique edge. By now, you hopefully have realized the difference between $50,000 a year or $50,000 a month is the edge.

A well-established pioneer in the industry of business had much to say about "the edge." He grew up with a Jewish background, similar to my upbringing, and he cultivated an impressive amount of value, leading to his extraordinary wealth and success. Mark Cuban, who many of you know from the entrepreneurial TV show, "Shark Tank," speaks passionately on the edge in his business book, *How to Win at the Sport of Business: If I Can Do It, You Can Do It.*

Below, I have selected a short excerpt from his book, one that greatly expanded my thinking as it pertains to success. I believe when describing the edge in detail, Cuban said it best;

The edge is getting so jazzed about what you do, you just spent 24 hours straight working on a project and you thought only a couple hours had passed.

The edge is knowing that you have to be the smartest guy in the room when you have your meeting and you are going to put in the effort to learn whatever you need to learn to get there.

The edge is knowing that when four girlfriends you have had in the last couple years asked you which was more important, them or your business, you gave the right answer.

The edge is knowing that you can fail and learn from it, and just get back up and in the game.

The edge is knowing that people think you're crazy, and they are right, but you don't care what they think.

The edge is knowing how to blow off steam a couple times a week, just so you can refocus on business.

The edge is knowing that you are getting to your goals and treating people right along the way, because as good as you can be, you are so focused that you need regular people around you to balance and help you.

The edge is being able to confidently call out someone on a business issue because you have done your homework.

The edge is recognizing when you are wrong and working harder to make sure it doesn't happen again.

The edge is being able to drill down to identify issues and problems and solve them before anyone knows they are there.

The edge is knowing that while everyone else is talking about nonsense like the "will to win" and how they know they can be successful, you are preparing yourself to compete so that you will be successful.

Business, like sports, is discipline and heart combined for something you believe in so deeply that it wouldn't matter what anyone else said or thought about you. It's days you get so engulfed and preoccupied with what you do that you forget to eat. It is the willingness to fail as many times as it takes until you achieve what it is you are going after. It is seeing the bigger picture of your life and working harder than anyone else until you fulfill its attainment. It is prioritizing what's important to you, including the relationships that will push you to stick with it. It is sacrificing a night out with your friends and investing that time on your personal goals. It's understanding that sacrifice in the short term is the price you pay for long-term success. I am not suggesting that you ditch your girlfriend who has supported you the last eight years, what I am saying is that you need to evaluate every single one of your relationships and make an honest observation of whether they are holding you back or pushing you forward.

I am where I am today because I continually failed, learned from mistakes, and got better. Don't quit on a bad day and compromise your chances to learn from it. Keep going, keep pushing, pivot when you need to, and don't be another spectator in the event of success. What you deposit in this moment and in the moments to follow will put in place a compound interest that nobody can devalue. Take the losses and level up your standards. Success is a sport much like any of the other games you play, and there are tough seasons and seasons where you rise above what you couldn't have fathomed you'd accomplish.

Everyone can play, but not everyone will win. Not because the capability is not there or cannot be developed, but because the willingness to show up and keep conditioning yourself is difficult. It takes dedication, and it's a daily decision you have to keep making over and over and over. Eventually, you will cross the goal line. Keep running!

ETHICS OF SUCCESS

"I've learned that people will forget what you said, people will forget what you did, but people will never forget how you made them feel."
– Maya Angelou

When I was growing up, I remember the moments my dad would set aside the time to talk to me about character and integrity. These were the conversations that developed much of who I am today, along with some of the core principles I discuss at my events and speaking engagements. Out of all the books, teachings, and lessons that I have learned about success, the conversations I have had with my father, carry the most weight. They helped me during the peak highs of my career, and they gave me strength to keep showing up in the lower moments, too.

When I reflect on some of those conversations, one in particular really stands out. My dad took me out for lunch one day to a steakhouse in Columbus. As our waiter arrived at our table with our food, I noticed across the table that my dad was talking to the server and had the most sincere smile on his face. My dad politely thanked our server, and we started to dig in. For some people, common etiquette is no big deal, it's a standard. Respect to my father, however, is connected to who he is. As we sat across from each other having lunch, he began to talk to me about impressions. Specifically, the kind that we leave on the people we come in contact with. He taught me that the measure of a person comes down to how they treat other people. Mother Teresa once stated, *"If we have no peace, it is because we have forgotten that we belong to each other."*

Out of all the things that separate one person from another, there is one abiding truth that diminishes our right to ever discriminate against others — that is our humanity. It would behoove you to understand that no matter how great your platform, there will be moments throughout your life where you must decrease before you can increase.

THE JANITOR AND THE CEO

My mom and my dad ran a successful insurance agency, which centered around people first. If you were to ask them what they believed to be the secret to their success, they would tell you, *"Make other people feel important."*

You can be ultra-confident and still treat the janitor the same way you treat the CEO.

"Make other people feel important, not belittled."

Before I dive in on the topic of humility, I would like to share something that I read by the author and speaker Simon Sinek. I had been speaking with a friend on the phone about Sinek's book, Leaders Eat Last. My friend had asked me to send him one of Sinek's speeches I'd mentioned to him, but I got distracted and spent the next 30 minutes looking at everything except for the speech. Have you ever done this? I admit this because to try and deny all the moments that our humanity has led us to participate in meaningless activities, would in fact defeat the purpose of this subject. I believe that our humanity goes hand in hand with our ability to have humility.

As I was scrolling through some recent nonsense, a post caught my attention, which read, "Confidence is to know that you are good at something. Arrogance is to entertain the idea that other people give a shit." You see, we can all agree that there is a healthy level of confidence that is necessary to achieve your goals. When people become too timid and passive about the things they desire in life, it can ultimately lead to a dangerous mindset of contempt. Confidence is knowing your worth, talents, abilities, and skills, but also knowing you are not better than anyone else.

In the house where I grew up, we were taught to believe in ourselves to the highest degree, but at the same time treat everyone with the same level of respect. Arrogance arises when we not only know that we add value, but we expect other people to recognize and act in a way that affirms it. Remember, in order to increase, we must often decrease. By decrease, I do not mean to succumb to a lower state of being and doing. I simply mean you and I will go farther in life if we conduct ourselves with compassion and empathy. We must strive to meet people at the level of understanding they might have, in order to bring them up and encourage them to pursue and participate in their shared spiritual inclination to grow and contribute.

The ability to do this and to be effective is what makes great leaders. Before I was 25 years old, I went from zero to a hundred in virtually every area of my life. My monthly paychecks were increasing exponentially, from a low three-figure income to well over six figures in a very short time frame. I was convinced that I was the greatest thing since Halo Top ice cream.

Eventually, the arrogant nature of that idea led me to a temporary downfall in my career. I had to learn some painful lessons during that time, for which I'm now grateful. If I could tell the younger, cockier version of myself one thing, it would be: *"Never get too self-righteous to clean your own toilets."* In other words, never live your life as though it would be beneath you to perform the duties of a janitor. The truth of the matter is that if any task or act of service is beneath you, the opportunity to work as a CEO will always be beyond you.

LEADERSHIP IS INFLUENCE

My dad always said, "Breathe belief into the people around you." One of the most simple, yet profound ways that we can make an impact on the world is to start with one person at a time. This sends out waves of good energy that touches people and places beyond the scope of what you and

I can see in our natural environment. Some people refer to it as a domino effect. I like to think that it's another powerful example of how the Law of Attraction is working in synch with our lives.

"Living with BTE (Big Time Energy)"

When you speak highly of another person, you open yourself up to opportunities for favor. This is a great look at one of the spiritual laws that govern our world. This is something that the top leaders and CEOs understand. But there is something more to be said about leadership, something remarkably pressing that we often don't stop to consider. Remember that Simon Sinek speech I told you about, the one I was diligently working to find before getting distracted? Well, this was actually a talk Sinek was giving about his book, Leaders Eat Last, and what that title meant.

In 2013, the New York Times had discussed photos of horrific scenes from terrorist shootings in Kenya. This particular discussion tugged at my heart for reasons you'll soon understand. In one of the pictures, Sinek recalled the image of a mother lying on top of her child to shield her from the bullets. He explained that this picture was in essence, exactly what leadership is about. It's putting the needs of others before our own. It's about sacrifice and service. It's a heart posture, not a title or a position.

When I made the decision to start writing this book, I wanted it to be a representation of the growth I have experienced over the past few years. I wanted it to be full of ideas and inspiration that I collected from people who came from all different walks of life. I wanted it to be an authentic representation of who I am, and how the information has compounded over time to become wisdom by way of application. I spent hours of my time in quiet contemplation and in-depth study so that this book would represent growth in every aspect of my life, including how I articulate my thoughts.

I did this with each and every topic I have addressed in this book. I asked myself difficult questions, which I have also included for you. Some of the questions I want you to consider, especially if you wish to be a successful leader, are:

• Are you more concerned with being impressive than you are influential?

• What are some of the ways that you can serve within your industry, family, etc.?

• Who are some of your favorite leaders?

• What is it that makes them great?

• How are you breathing belief into others?

We have many excellent examples of leadership throughout history. Some of these people are names that if mentioned in conversation, you'd recognize. People like John C. Maxwell, Nelson Mandela, Jocko Willink, Jim Collins, and others. There is a long list of names that you and I may never hear about. Perhaps, your name would make that list.

REAL BIG MONEY ENERGY

We celebrate my wife's birthday in February. This past year, we decided to spend the entire month of February traveling to different countries around the world. Our most recent trip ended in a visit to different parts of Africa. Out of all the countries in the world, Africa holds a special place in our hearts. We felt connected to the people, the land, and the culture in a way that cannot be reduced to words.

One of our first destinations was Kenya, where we got to experience wildlife up close and personal with an African safari experience. From Kenya, we traveled on a small plane to Tanzania, where we landed in a dirt field. From the plane, we were picked up and escorted to where we would be staying. At that time, I had only heard about Kenya in light of tabloids and hearsay. I didn't really know what to expect, and the experience is one that has forever changed me, in the best of ways.

During the drive, I struck up a conversation with our driver. I was interested in their way of life, and I was trying to understand what it was about this place that tugged at my spirit. During our conversation, I learned that the working class may only earn somewhere between U.S.$200 and $500 a month. I was told that it is a luxury to have a kitchen or a bathroom in the homes of their communities. The thing that captivated me about the people in Africa was the genuine joy within their communities and villages. We were blown away by the hospitality, generosity, compassion, and their overall attitude, but the joy had an authenticity that is hard to come by.

As we got to meet with some of the different people who were helping to accommodate our stay, we learned a lot about their culture. As my wife and I sat across from each other for dinner one night, two things came to mind. The first was a quote from Sinek's book, Leaders Eat Last, and the second was a man who just about every leader across the world knows of. Sinek wrote, *"We are not victims of our situations. We are the architects of it."*

It occurred to me that the joy within the communities of the people was relative to their perspective. They weren't preoccupied by the noise of social media, and they weren't trying to Keep up with the Kardashians. Their lives existed only in the present moment, surrounded by families and community. They were interested in serving their neighbor and accommodating the guests in their country. They understood that it was a joy to serve, and it was quite literally their way of putting food on the table. They were not victims to life, they were architects. They were creating the most of every moment, grateful for what most of us consider the small things. To them, however, they were big.

The second thought that came to mind was by Nelson Mandela. He left a mark in this world that no man can erase. He transformed an entire nation, and his leadership reached different parts of the world. Furthermore, his wisdom impacted generations and will continue to do so. None of his accomplishments, however, was handed to him or made easy. Before becoming the first black president of South Africa in 1994, Nelson Mandela spent 27 years in prison. In reading Mandela's autobiography, I learned how much of this man's dynamic perspective on life has fundamentally impacted how you and I discuss leadership.

Mandela also had profound insight on the power of perspective, the same insight that is still very much alive within the communities among African people. Mandela wrote, *"As I walked out the door toward the gate that would lead to my freedom, I knew if I didn't leave my bitterness and hatred behind, I'd still be in prison."* He was no longer concerned about living in the past. He would go on to spend the rest of his life making a change that would outlast his time on Earth. He would go on to leave a legacy as one of the greatest leaders this world has known. In his autobiography, A Long Walk to Freedom, he writes about leadership, *"A leader is like a shepherd. He stays behind the flock, letting the most nimble go out ahead, whereupon the others follow, not realizing that all along they are being directed from behind."*

Humility often looks much like leading from the back. This is why it is imperative for people to continue to move forward, beyond what they are able to see taking place, beyond the setbacks, beyond the people who may have burned you in the past, and beyond the stories that may be holding you back from creating the life you desire. Remember, success is a mindset. Humility is a heart posture. Perspective is a choice. Our experience in Africa left us with remarkable memories, and the energy of the people was something that money can't buy.

When you're leading organizations in an influential position, people look up to you and follow you. Eventually, if you're arrogant and cocky, people will begin to turn on you and run away from you. I've learned that no one wants to follow arrogance and ego, the two ingredients that make cockiness.

I wish somebody had told me that no role ever said, "One must be cocky in order to be rich." You want to be supremely confident and know exactly who you are and where you're going, but remain humble and give all the credit away. You see, in the last 24 months, I've made more money than the first six years of my career. When I launched my third company, I told myself that no matter how big the company got or how much money I was making, I would remain in a humble spirit, give all the credit away, praise and love others, and never think that I was better than anyone else.

When you operate with a spirit of humility, people will want to follow you, and they'll respect you even more. The greatest compliments I get professionally is when people tell me that I'm the same as I was when I was 21 and broke, a.k.a. humble.

Take my advice here: You don't need to be a narcissist to become rich and successful. Whoever said "Nice guys finish last" can kiss my ass—it's not true. Good and humble people finish first. I challenge you to be loud, proud, excited, have posture, conviction, unwavering belief, and exude ultra-confidence. And at the same time, know you're no better than any other human being. Regardless of income, material possessions, etc., people are people. We are all God's children, and the highest form of creation.

One of the reasons I've been able to earn well over $30 million at 30 years of age is because of my BIG TIME ENERGY!
Let me explain. Whether it's 2 a.m. or 2 p.m., I am always vibrating high and excited about life and what it is I'm doing! You may say, "Well what's the big deal here?" ENERGY IS EVERYTHING. Yes — ENERGY IS EVERYTHING!!! Everything we do in our life is affected by the amount of ENERGY we invest into it.

When I got into real estate at 18, the reason why they gave me a shot, even though I knew nothing about real estate, was because of my contagious BIG TIME ENERGY. I've realized that most people have trashy energy. Most people walking around downtown Austin, Miami, and London, acting as if their life is terrible and running around with this "poor me"/victim mentality. If you mope around with your head down, angry, upset, and negative, I'll be the first to tell you that no one is going to want to hire you, work with you, or follow you. Why would they? People want to follow and be around people who are EXCITED about life, a.k.a. have BIG TIME ENERGY! BIG TIME ENERGY is the feeling you get when you're around someone who's absolutely crushing it at life, exuding massive self-confidence, and is always talking about his or her vision of the future. You can only get BIG TIME ENERGY when you're fully focused and committed on turning your dreams into realities.

Here are some ways to operate with BIG TIME ENERGY —

1. Don't be afraid to step into the unknown and take a chance.
Listen, life is short. In fact, it's very short. It feels like yesterday that I was an 18-year-old kid at ASU in a dorm room dreaming of becoming a millionaire, and now, today, I'm writing to you as just that — a millionaire, 30 times over. How did I get here? What did I do differently? One of the things I've always done is TAKE RISKS.

Starting my own business at 21, risking my name, reputation, and credibility so early on was a huge risk. Opting out of an internship my junior year of college in order to build my "small business" was a risk. Leaving a company in 2015 after they paid me $1,600,000 was a huge risk! Partnering with a company in 2016 that 99 out of 100 people told me not to, and that it would ruin my career, was an insane risk! So, how do we know which risks to take? It's a FEELING you get. The same FEELING I got when I met my future wife, the same FEELING I had when I shook hands with the CEO I'd partner with, that FEELING is the intuition. We all have it inside of us; it is always trying to steer us in the right direction. If it FEELS right, pull the trigger. If it doesn't, walk away. Taking risks early on in my career has had a lot to do with my success.

2. Decide that success is important.
On your journey to becoming who you're destined to be, you'll be faced with many decisions, and you'll need to CHOOSE SUCCESS over many other things in your life. You're not reading this book to earn $75,000 a year. You're reading this book to earn $75,000+ a

week.

The top one percent will all tell you about the magnitude of sacrifices they made to get to where they are today. You must **DECIDE** that **SUCCESS IS IMPORTANT** to you and operate with a certain degree of commitment—worthy of becoming massively successful. When you wake up inspired and go to sleep inspired, you will create BIG TIME ENERGY throughout your whole body. That's how it works. When you're fired up and excited, you will exude BIG TIME ENERGY (BTE)!!

3. Get around other people with BIG TIME ENERGY!!
If you're reading this chapter, you're probably thinking, '*Listen, I understand what you're saying, but my life sucks right now, and it's tough to have this type of energy.*'

First off, I understand — and I understand there is something you can do about it, so you, too, can have BTE and begin to elevate your life. Getting around other people who are pumped about life, winning at high levels, and are operating with BTE is a great way for some of that to rub off on you. One of my mentors told me, "Alex, your network will soon become your net worth" — meaning, if you want to win, get around winners. If you want more BTE, get around people who have it. Attend events, seminars, watch YouTube videos, pay for mentorship or membership courses of people with BTE! Also, if you can physically get close to someone with BTE, do it. One tip for getting close to someone with BTE is finding ways to provide value and service to them. GETTING and OPERATING with BIG TIME ENERGY is essential for your success!! The best part is that anyone can live with BIG TIME ENERGY!

FOLLOW ONE COURSE UNTIL SUCCESSFUL

"The world steps aside for the man who knows where he is going."
– James Allen, in As a Man Thinketh

When I first began building up knowledge within my industry, I had a great opportunity to travel from state to state, learning about the business. Whether it was prospecting people to build up a team or hosting events, I clocked in a lot of hours behind the wheel. Road trips gave me plenty of time to sort through my thoughts. Gone are the times where you had no option but to stop at a gas station and purchase a little pamphlet with a paper map, pulling over multiple times to make sure you were still headed toward your destination. In a lot of ways, the technological advances in our society have given us practical tools to be more efficient; particularly with GPS applications that are available. How many of you rely on your phone to make it back from your local grocery store? If you answered yes, it's time to work on your situational awareness skills. While living in Arizona, my wife and I decided we would take a short road trip from Scottsdale, Arizona, to see the red rock hiking trails in Sedona.

Our spontaneous road trip had me reminiscing on the early stages of my career, where for several hours it was just me and the open road. The car ride from Scottsdale to Sedona is about two-and-a-half hours, which goes by fairly quickly. We were almost halfway there when I caught myself looking in the rear-view mirror as I scanned the road behind us to make sure we weren't breaking any speeding laws. As we coasted down the freeway, I thought to myself, "I wonder how the heck people could arrive safely to their destination if they focused only on what was behind them instead of in front of them." Such a dumb thought, I know — except this is exactly how many people will arrive at their future destination, staring at a reflection of their past.

"EMPIRE STATE OF MIND"

If you have ever had the chance to take a road trip or travel across the country with some of your closest friends or with your toddlers, you know that the key to a successful trip is a good throwback playlist with some of your favorite songs.

If you're anything like me, your playlist will consist of artists like Drake, Maluma, Big Sean, G-Eazy, Lil Baby, J Balvin, and maybe you'll throw in some old school Whitney Houston and get fired up. Come on, now, I know there are a few of you reading this book who can turn up a song and envision yourself up on stage as a famous singer. If you really want to have a good time, turn up the music, wait until everyone is singing at the top of their lungs, and then hit that power button. It is the fastest way to kill someone's dreams of being a superstar, unless, of course, you can hit the high notes.

I believe it was a well-known Greek philosopher by the name of Plato who said,

"Music is a moral law. It gives a soul to the universe, wings to the mind, flight to the imagination, a charm to sadness, and life to everything."

Earlier, I spoke about some of my favorite athletes and what they had to share on the subject of success. Whether it was their methods during championship games, their mindsets both on the court and off the court, or their personal beliefs about success, many of these ultra-successful people were once ordinary people from humble beginnings.

Shawn Corey Carter, born December 4, 1969, in Brooklyn, New York, became one of the world's most famous rappers, Jay-Z. He was an artist known for far more than his lyrical capabilities and is today also one of the most prominent figures in business. Jay-Z and his wife Beyoncé have a combined net worth of over $1 billion, and it is not only because of their success in the music industry. When I heard his story, he too became a person I aspired to learn about. I wanted to know about his philosophies and what took him to the top. I wanted to understand the principles that led this man to be one of the few rappers inducted into the Rock & Roll Hall of Fame, and, beyond that, a well-accomplished entrepreneur and investor.

A person's circumstances, as well as their upbringing, have nothing to do with the destination they will arrive at. Although it is easy to assume that circumstances play a big role in success, it is certainly not the truth. Success results from decisions and disciplines that are executed and acted upon regularly. Although your choices can seem insignificant, they have a compounded effect on your success. Jay-Z understood this, and he showed his understanding when he shared his story and spoke about the lessons he had learned throughout his experiences. He recorded his first album at 26 years old. This is the same man who was told by an uncle that he would never be as good as LL Cool J.

Many of you who are reading this may not yet have turned 21, and you still feed into the idea that it's too late for you or that you missed the opportunity to make something great for yourself. The greatest tragedy for most young people is not that they fail a million times, but that they never learn from their failures. It is not a tragedy to grow up in an environment that you did not choose; it is a tragedy to insist on staying there.

I talked about Jay-Z not because he had a unique series of miracles that led to his monumental achievement. If you listen to his music and if you take the time to research his story, you would learn that he grew up in the Marcy Projects. He experienced violence, drug dealings, and the repercussions of that lifestyle firsthand. He had to apply himself to get out of an environment he was born into. He knew that to stay there would be a decision he made daily, and he understood the same is true about success. His story was a series of events and decisions that led him to where he is today.

Excellence is not an abstract idea born from extreme poverty or extreme wealth. Excellence is a prioritized effort to push against the status quo, the stereotypes, and the systemic stupidity that cultivates failure-type societal standards. The decisions that led Jay-Z from the Marcy Projects to Madison Square Garden is the same thing that can lead you from where you are now to where you want to be. Mindset.

"Jay Z – from rags to riches with determination & quality"

"I believe excellence is being able to perform at a high level over and over."
– Jay-Z

"I'M STARTING WITH THE MAN IN THE MIRROR"

On June 25, 2009, an announcement that headlined every major media outlet across the world shocked many. The "King of Pop" had died of an alleged drug overdose, shattering the hearts of all those who had been impacted by his music. The death of Michael Jackson had an impact that stretched beyond the world of entertainment, causing people to mourn his loss all around the world. Jackson began his career as an entertainer at the age of five. His success is how the world remembers him, but the genuine tragedy of his life was the distorted legacy he left the world with. From a young age, Jackson was under scrutiny. His life was always making news headlines, but it was not in a good way. He was eventually found innocent of the accusations that had surfaced throughout the years, but he left this world before getting to experience relief from the negative publicity.

Now, Michael Jackson changed the game in music, and his entire life can teach us a very important message. How you see yourself is what matters most. At the core of every failure, and of every success, lies a belief about who you are. If Jay-Z had listened to his uncle and accepted the belief that he would never be as good as the rappers and artists that had gone before him, his actions would have remained consistent with a character that somebody else had created. Instead, he had determined at a young age that his perception was his prerogative, and somebody else's personal projections did not have to become something that he identified with.

We can find the key to success in an honest evaluation of what you believe about yourself, known in psychology as self-image. Whether a person admits it, the first glance you get of yourself when you brush your teeth in the morning is an ill-defined and surface level idea of your self-image. In fact, your reflection is merely what is consciously recognizable. Your self-image is the unconscious blueprint that you have on hand at all times that guides you to a destination in the future. You can think of it as the internal GPS, the map system within your mind that takes you to your destination.

At the beginning of this chapter, I wrote of a road trip in Arizona that my wife and I took from Scottsdale to Sedona. Before we had left Scottsdale, I made sure that we had input the address of the hotel we had booked our reservation with. Imagine if I had input the incorrect address and location. Not only would we have wasted time and gas money, there was a solid possibility that we would have completely detoured and ended up in an area far less exciting and potentially dangerous. I am not suggesting that a little off-road adventure is entirely bad. What I am saying, however, is that not knowing exactly where you are going can cause severe problems. This is the reason many people get off course in their life. They become too engulfed in distractions and eventually arrive at a destination by default, instead of by design.

The fact of the matter is that I would never arrive at my intended destination if I only attempted to change the roads I was taking. In order to arrive at the correct place, I would have to have the correct address on my phone. Your mind works like a GPS system, and if you want to make it to a destination that you input by design, sometimes you need to change the default settings. While challenges in life arrive without consulting your agenda, there are some that can be a little more difficult to overcome. These types of challenges are complex because they are attached to an idea you have about who you are, and so you find that you're wading in problems that essentially have to do with your self-image and your personality traits. Had any training in any of that?

Maxwell Maltz, author of *Psycho-Cybernetics*, was one of the first researchers to explain the effects of the self-image. A large part of his career was as a cosmetic surgeon, consulting with patients who had issues with their physical image. Whether it was victims of a tragic accident or patients who were concerned about a particular genetic abnormality, the discoveries that Maltz details in his book go far beyond his career as a plastic surgeon. His teachings have inspired many experts in personal growth, motivational speakers, life coaches, sports psychologists, and successful entrepreneurs.

Maltz's writing provides us with an incontestable truth about the perceptions that can imprison us when we do not properly address them. Maltz writes,

"This self-image is our own conception of the 'sort of person I am.' It has been built up from our own beliefs about ourselves. But most of these beliefs about ourselves have unconsciously been formed from our past experiences, our successes and failures, our humiliations, our triumphs, and the way other people have reacted to us, especially in early childhood. From all these we mentally construct a 'self' (or a picture of a self)."

You can think of this internal picture of yourself as the map coordinates that take you to a destination. It is the address that you will eventually arrive at, either by design or by default. In a time when we did not have the technology to make our lives easier, we probably would have pulled over and asked for directions in the event we had gone off course. Back in the day, the response might have been ,"Where are you trying to go?" Today, you would probably get some strange looks if you did that, but if you were lost, you would need a good sense of direction to get you back on course.

Some of you might feel as if every time you try to change a habit of behavior in your life, you have difficulty remaining consistent. I believe it could be time for you to consult your internal GPS. The reality concerning your personal success is that before you consult with a mentor or stop to ask for directions, you need to know where you are headed. You need to double check that you are truly headed toward your desired destination, instead of the destination programmed by your default setting. Before you hit the road running, make sure you know where you're headed and make sure you have a good playlist for the ride.

Some of the most memorable moments in our lives are permanently ingrained in our memory, much like a song. Some of your thoughts can even emerge from your subconscious as song lyrics. As I glanced up at the rear-view mirror, looking back at the road behind me, a tune shortly followed my thoughts:

> *"I'm starting with the man in the mirror*
> *I'm asking him to change his ways*
> *And no message could have been any clearer*
> *If you want to make the world a better place*
> *Take a look at yourself, and then make a change."*

GOD'S GREATEST GIFT: THE IMAGINATION

The imagination is the most marvelous, inconceivably powerful force in the universe. Look around — notice your environment and the intricate details that surround you. If you live in an apartment, stop for a moment and examine your living space. Perhaps you are still in school and currently living in the campus housing wherever you are; look at that environment and study it. Understand that everything you see began in the mind of someone else. Everything, including you. At some point, mom and dad had to think about you before you popped out nine months later. Knowing that to be true, we understand that everything that shows up in the physical world first begins in the spiritual world, a.k.a., the imagination. Our ability to create an image in our mind and have it manifest as tangible reality is the gift of imagination. God intended for us to use this gift and experience the fullness of its power. We are unlike every other creation and every other life form. We can visualize and create our life by first creating an image in our mind.

One of the first steps to achieving and getting the life you want is to use your imagination and let your imagination run wild. What do I mean by that? Take a second and imagine your dream car, imagine your dream house. What does it look like? Who's in it? What cars are in the driveway? What planes are you flying in? I've been imagining one of our dream homes since I was a little kid.

My imagination was always going crazy, and I remember my teacher telling me in school, "Snap out of it, Alex. Pay attention. Stop looking out the window." Little did they know – and little did I know – that I was using my imagination to create the life I was going to live in the future. Everything I've ever imagined in my life has eventually come to pass. You can do the same thing. You have the same ability to manifest anything you want in your life.

Use your imagination! Our minds think in pictures. Tonight, before you go to sleep in Topeka, Kansas, or Tulsa, Oklahoma, or Beijing, China, take a second and let your imagination run wild and imagine life as you would like it to be. See the life you imagine—vividly see it in concrete, specific detail, and then feel as if you're in that moment. Before I was driving the actual car, I was driving it in my mind. Before I was wearing the real jewelry, I was wearing the jewelry in my mind. Before I could help pay off my parents' home and buy my mom a car and buy my sister a car, and buy my friends and family whatever it is they wanted, I saw all of that happening in my mind first. Even when I was broke at 18, eating ramen noodles in the dorm room, I used my imagination to make a clear picture of exactly where I was going.

Your belief system is composed of the things that you see, the things that you hear, and the things that you experience. Make sure you're saturating your mind with images and pictures of what you want, e.g., that dream car, that dream home, that ideal bank account. You must have a vision for your life and where you want to end up. In life, you don't get what you want, you get what you picture, and what you see with your imagination. So use this powerful creative force within and picture the life you desire. Turn your dreams into reality!

Most people don't use their imagination constructively. They use it destructively—they imagine what they don't want. We've got to consciously and deliberately imagine what we do want. Understand that this is an inclusion-based universe. Everything is about inclusion, so whatever we see, both positive and negative, will be the very things that we attract into our lives.

As you finish this chapter, I would like you to grab a pen and begin to answer the question: "What do I really want?"

Write it in the present tense, which you can reference in the future. Build a vision of what you would like to accomplish between now and the end of the month or year, and repetitively make a written description of that vision.

Vision is going to direct your life, if you let it. Use it constructively and see what you want. You are a creative being. You are, in fact, creating every moment of your life. You created your image of yourself, your present job, what's in your bank account, and your relationships with your friends. You even create new cells and a new body every few months. Whether you're aware of it, you are tapped into the energy of the creative flow of the Universe. It's literally flowing to and through you, and if you become more aware of this creative energy inside of you, it will change your life in phenomenal ways.

Unfortunately, when we were little kids, our parents may have stifled our imaginations and creativity. Your parents or teachers may have told you to pay attention, like they told me. Or maybe they said you'd never be a lawyer, singer, entrepreneur, or whatever you longed to be. You were a child, so you obeyed them and believed what they said. And so you learned to let your dreams go. But now, you know better, and you can go beyond that. You see, you are divinely guided by Spirit at all times, and Spirit is perfect—it makes no mistakes. When you have a strong desire to express or create something, know that the feeling is divinely guided. There is something in you that wants to grow! When a big idea comes to mind, you have the choice of keeping it alive by letting your imagination flow, or dismissing it and remaining stuck in fear.

Trusting the perfection that lives within you is the key. Ever since I was 16 years old, I really burned into my subconscious mind the image and the idea of the things I wanted. Many people study the Law of Attraction and the Law of Vibration, and they want that car, that house, that rank at a company, or that future partner. It's one thing just to want something, but it's another thing to get emotionally tied into it. It starts with our belief system, and our beliefs are made up of the things we see, the things we hear, and the things we experience. So even at 16, watching Entourage on HBO, I put myself in Vinnie Chase's body. I put myself in Paris, France, walking around the Eiffel Tower with my friends, and then seven years later, I found myself in Paris, strolling by the Eiffel Tower with my friends. I put myself in the feeling of when they were sitting in Barcelona, Spain, eating tapas and drinking margaritas with a bunch of guys and girls and then, seven years later, I'm in Barcelona, having fun and celebrating life in Barcelona.

Get invested with the things that you desire, and do that by using your imagination, turning your mind into video projection software, to where your future life is being shown to you. It's one thing to want it, and it's another thing to get into the harmonious vibration of that. You do it through your belief system, emotions, and becoming completely submerged and obsessed with the idea at a subconscious level.

"Going there mentally," stems from, "Act as if." Some people say don't act as if, because they feel they're lying or overembellishing. For me, acting as if, acting like the person I want to become, was one of the biggest triggers of growth in my career. When I was 21 years old, I acted as if I were already a millionaire. I was acting as if the results that I desired were already here in the physical world. Go there mentally. Whatever you want, you can go there.

If the goal is to make $10,000 a month, if the goal is to make $50,000 a month, whatever the goal is – maybe it's to lose ten pounds, maybe it's to build a better relationship with your significant other – whatever the goal is, there is a place for your to picture it in your imaginatiopn. Then ask yourself: "How would that person act? Talk, walk, eat, sleep, drink? What time would they wake up in the morning? What time would they go to sleep at night?" You must act as if you're already in possession of the good that you desire. I want you to go there today. Whatever that goal is, go there mentally and then become that person right now. You must build the image, build the idea, build the result in the spiritual world of imagination before it can manifest into the physical universe. Go there in your imagination, and think, act, and feel as if it's already done.

Part III

FINAL REMARKS

This Part of this book is dedicated to my mentors; to my smart, beautiful, and amazing wife; to my little sister; and to my incredible parents. You all are my greatest inspirations. I would also like to, once again, recognize and honor my mentor and my friend, Bob Proctor. Your memory and your work will continue to be a light and a legacy for generations to come. These are the people who have fundamentally changed my life.

They gave me much of the passion I have for helping people around the world. They instilled in me the power of belief. They taught me how to expect more of myself than I do of others, and their legacies will continue to touch millions around the world.

ABOVE ALL ELSE, LOVE DEEPLY!

"The power of a glance has been so much abused in love stories that it has come to be disbelieved in.
Few people dare now to say that two beings have fallen in love because they have looked at each other.
Yet it is in this way that love begins, and in this way only."

– Victor Hugo

One night, late after a business event, I called one of my closest friends. We got to talking about life and experiences, and he said, "You know, Alex, you have to find some time to get away from what you do and just experience life."

I shrugged it off and thought to myself, "What does he know? I have traveled to hundreds of countries all over the world, and he has barely left America, or even the state he was born in." But I realized that my friend was right. I had spent all of my time traveling from place to place, living out of a suitcase only to get on an early morning flight and on to the next city.

It dawned on me that, although I had been flying in and out of countries for years, I didn't actually visit those countries. My usual experience consisted of going to the business event venue, to the hotel lobby, back to my room, and then to the airport for my next business event. If I was feeling fired up, I'd check out a restaurant that was recommended by locals or other leaders within the company. Most of the time, I was entertaining potential business prospects with some drinks and appetizers by the hotel pool. There were only a handful of times that I took an extra day to explore a country, and by handful I mean that one time when I went to visit the fabulous cathedrals in Rome.

My buddy knew that I rarely broke away from business, and as much as I didn't want to admit it, he made a good point. Sure, staying in the top resorts and flying first class all over the world had its benefits, but I couldn't really call myself cultured simply because I had tons of air miles and great hotel accommodations.

I decided to take his advice and have a little fun. I was staying in London at the time. I made a few phone calls and found myself at a nightclub known for its atmosphere and vibrancy. It was a little past 1 a.m. when I saw this girl walking across the room from a distance. I was having a good time, feeling pretty confident, and I decided to take a chance on "experiencing life" like other people. I stood up and walked directly toward her, and I remember thinking, "I'll introduce myself, ask her name, and see what happens."

Have you ever heard it said that everybody has a plan — until they get punched in the face? Well, I was that guy. I didn't get punched in the face, but the moment I stood in front of her, the conversation that proceeded was anything but, "Hi, how are you." Instead of the normal opening lines guys use every day all over the world, something else came to me. In a moment of bravery, I said to her, "I'm going to marry you."

There are probably a number of things going through your head right now, ranging from, "I'm embarrassed for you" to "Dude, good for you!" Think about the Nike slogan, and "Just Do It!" That's really how it went down, just past 1 a.m. My future self manifested itself in the most casual way, and I told the woman of my dreams to stop searching — we're getting married!

I wish I could claim that the following steps I took were in my favor, but they weren't. In fact, she completely blew me off that night. The Prince Charming in me, however, took the liberty of sorting through her friends' pages on Instagram, and I finally found her webpage. Eventually, I convinced her to have dinner with me in Stockholm, Sweden.

As the night progressed, it became the second best night of my life. I felt things I had never felt before, and I flew back home with a certainty that she was most likely "The One." We remained in contact off and on until I saw her again in Europe a year later. We spent some more time together in London, where we had met. From London, we went to the Greek vacation city of Mykonos, on the Greek island of Mykonos.

I knew that I couldn't envision my life without her. She was smart and amazingly cultured, in ways unknown to me, and she had confidence about who she was and what she wanted out of life. It felt as though I had known her my whole life, and after many serious conversations, I convinced her to leave her family, friends, career, school, and continent and move to America. Somehow, some way, she did. A few months later, I got down on one knee and asked her a question that would forever change my life, in the best ways a man can be changed. She said yes, and to this day, I am eternally grateful. She is absolutely my Number One Priority, and I love her for it.

I am no romance novelist, but I'm sharing this with you for a few reasons. The first is the power of relationship. I don't mean the surface-level relationships that reject commitment and lack transparency — I want to talk to you about real, solid connection. I am not an expert, but I do know that we humans are wired for connection. We are made to thrive in relationships, and if you find yourself constantly running on empty and unable to see life in an empowering way, the first place to start is with your relationships.

This chapter is important because the quality of your life directly comes down to the health and vibrancy of your relationships, especially your intimate relationships.

Before we dive in, I also want to assure you that what you will learn in this chapter is applicable across the board. It holds true for business partnerships, friendships, personal relationships such as family, co-workers, and intimate relationships. Relationships are fundamental to our lives, and if you were to be incredibly honest with yourself, you would find it true that if there is no joy in your interactions with others, especially the ones closest to you, then it would be hard to experience joy in any other area of your life, specifically the kind of joy that leads to fulfillment. Tony Robbins made a great point when he said, "If you aren't happy in your relationships, then you aren't happy!" It's really that simple, and if you are single, I'm glad that you have made it this far in the book. This is as applicable to you as it is to anyone else, so don't get ahead of yourself. What makes a relationship great? What creates the difference within relationships that allows us to communicate effectively with our partner, or those within our inner circle?

KNOW WHAT YOU WANT!

The problem with today's society is that we have more people who know what they don't want than what they do want! They can give you an entire list of all the things they don't like and all the things that bother them. I often hear people claim that this is a result of high standards, but really it's immaturity. You have to start with what you want, and that comes easy to you when you have spent some time figuring out who you are.

If you have made an effort to apply the concepts in this book, making a list of what you look for in people should come easy to you. You can start by getting good at making decisions. From there, it takes some introspective time considering the role that you play in your relationships, whether the majority of them inspire you or make you feel insecure.

Ownership changes the game. I knew what I wanted in a woman. I knew that I wanted my future wife to be a high-level entrepreneur, full of energy, goals, and an internal clarity of the type of life she wanted to live. I knew I needed someone who could support me 24/7 and make every effort to understand me despite the messy parts of my humanity. This is the power of intention. If your relationships seem infiltrated by a spirit of negativity, constant complaining, strife, animosity, etc., ask questions such as: What story am I telling about their intentions? What sort of assumptions am I making about what they are thinking and feeling?

Most relationships don't fail due to a lack of love. They fail due to an inability to focus. Focus on the truth instead of your truth. (I touched on this principle earlier. It goes hand in hand with the stories that we tell ourselves.)

Sometimes, people inevitably get caught up in their own mental narrative, and when any sort of discomfort arises, their trash becomes their truth. This is why it is important to know what you want, and more often than not it comes down to two thing:. a list that you have considered based on your unique desires and vision, as well as a very important question — Do you want to prove a point? Or do you want to understand? When you silence the ego and try to see life from the perspective of another person, you get compassion and empathy. Simultaneously, that choice is made out of love.

"What am I getting out of this, anyway?"

WHAT ARE YOU CONTRIBUTING?

People tend to ask: What am I getting from this?

You must learn to ditch this question. Sure, relationships must be full of contribution on both ends, but that can't and won't happen until you've established the answers to the earlier questions above. Relationships are about service. Service is also applicable in the chapter on leadership, titled Ethics of Success. This, however, is a different kind of leadership. You are responsible for yourself, which you'll find time and time again. Taking responsibility for your actions, behaviors, expectations, stories and assumptions directly affects the person you spend your life with. It also affects other relationships. We have raised an entire generation under fabricated clichés that have very little to do with sanity.

In fact, these clichés, fairy tales, and unrealistic slogans about life and love are a breeding ground for unmet expectations. My personal favorite is, "Relationships are 50/50. It's give and take." While this advice may have come wrapped in a bubble of good intentions made to console the wounded spirit, it's overrated and illiterate. A 50/50 relationship is one in which one person constantly keeps tabs on the other person. It's usually centered around the question, "What am I getting from this?" This is a recipe for disaster, because while you're focusing on how much weight someone else is pulling, you aren't investing that time taking ownership for your own load.

Life is complicated, and that manifests in your relationships when you do the opposite of everything you have learned in this book. You start to become the victim not only in your life, but also in your relationships. It becomes an endless cycle of making other people in charge of your happiness when most people have a hard time remembering to brush their teeth in the morning.

Whoever coined the term, "my other half," did our society a great disservice. I don't know about you, but I don't want a half person. I want someone who is whole. They were good before they met me, but because they are at a place in their life where they know their worth, they desire to show up and do life with me. It's a different level of commitment.

The 50/50 relationship rule has failed people for several reasons. You must get rid of the outlook that says, "What is so-and-so bringing to the table?" This robs you of your divine intention to serve others in a meaningful way, in a way that brings you joy and fulfillment. If you constantly show up in your relationships under the impression that somebody owes you something, your life is going to be a mess. Your relationships are going to be a mess. Know what you want, and know what it is that you can bring to the table.

Love without expectation. There will be highs and lows that wreck our plans, and if you don't have emotional stability, you make no room for growth. Stability in relationships is understanding. It's navigating the issues that arise when experiences don't match the expectations. Nobody should ever complete you, as awesome as that sounds. You need to be complete, and do life with people who have learned the value of that concept. Relationships are 100/100, or it won't be long before that relationship becomes a relation-shit. A quality relationship starts with a quality question that armors itself with extreme ownership: What am I bringing to the table?

REAL, NOT REHEARSED!

I dedicate this entire section to my incredible wife because without her, the core principles that I discuss with you would carry no real weight in my life.

This next topic is just as valuable to intimate relationships, as well as the relationship that you have with yourself, your family, your co-workers, and your close friends. Be real, not rehearsed. With social media nowadays, we're inundated with the "idealistic" male or female to be with, or which real theme is getting the most views, and so many other rehearsed versions of reality. The issue is that 99 percent of photos and videos we see are exactly that – rehearsed. I want to emphasize that if your desire is to be an influencer or content creator of any kind, that's fantastic. I am not shading people who make a living off of this kind of thing, I am, however, saying that we need to be careful not to misconstrue social media status for real life.

As someone who has built a huge portion of my personal brand while leveraging social media, I can tell you that there is more to influence than meets the eye. I also think it's important that people understand the difference between being an influencer (career choice/job description) and being influential. While this topic can be controversial, it's relevant to the world we are living in. One is a job that has people doing all kinds of things to inspire a mass of people to buy into whatever they are promoting. The other asks a deeper question, that is: 'What kind of influence do I want to have on this world? How am I contributing in a meaningful way to the lives of the people around me?' When people aren't careful about separating the two, sometimes the focus in our real life, personal connections with people, get traded for a counterfeit version that carries many other issues. This can be a threat to intimacy, and a costly one at that.

We have to get certain and intentional about who we are and how we are going to show up in our relationships, and we must learn to manage our expectations so that we don't lose sight of what matters. The images we see online are photoshopped and although yes, you want an attractive partner and someone you're sexually attracted to, let's be real: we all grow older and eventually, a lot of our beauty will fade. So, we should seek someone who's beautiful inside as well as outside.

Before meeting my wife, I remember making a list of what was important to me in a partner. Although I lost that sheet of paper, I still remember what I desired. This list has no order of importance.

- Sharp / smart / educated
- Compassionate and loving
- Desires to have children and start a family in the future
- Loves me for me not just because of who I am or what I have
- Prioritizes health by leading an active lifestyle, stimulating the mind by learning new things, and taking special care to be considerate of what she's putting in her body to nourish herself for longevity
- Desires to explore the world and its various different cultures
- Open to having a faith-based relationship/believing in something bigger than our humanity
- Darker hair, features, etc.
- Drop-dead gorgeous

I suggest you make a list of exactly what you want in your future partner. We already know we attract what we think about and write down. Let this person's traits, personality, physical beauty, etc. become one of the dominating thoughts of your mind, and you will send energy into the Universe, and this person will show up. I'm living proof of this.

Here are some things you can do to attract the person you want to spend the rest of your life with:

1. Write down exactly what you want in the person and do it with excruciating detail.

2. Create a vision board of what this person will look like and who they'll emulate physically. This may sound crazy, but everything I've put on my wall I've attracted into my life. From my 2020 Rolls Royce to living in a $8,000,000 penthouse in Miami. Trust me — find pictures of what they'll look like, places you'll go together, events you'll attend, what you'll be wearing, what you talk about, etc. This works.

3. Increase the intensity of your attracting powers by becoming the best version of yourself. Eat clean, work out, read books, focus on your goals and dreams, etc. WE ATTRACT WHO WE ARE. If you want a fit person, get fit. If you want an educated person, get educated. Allow yourself to grow, change, and evolve into your best self.

4. Adopt an attitude of gratitude. A great way to increase your happiness is by being thankful and grateful for the things already in your life.

Listen, I didn't really believe in true love for close to 29 years. I thought it was only in the movies or for old-school people. Today, I can confidently say, "It's real, it exists, and love can be yours!!! When you're with the right person, your money and success will multiply!!!"

LIFE, LEGACY, AND THE PURSUIT OF GREATNESS

"Those times when you get up early and you work hard;
those times when you stay up late and you work hard;
those times when you don't feel like working, you're too tired,
you don't want to push yourself, but you do it anyway; that is
actually the dream.
That's the dream. It's not the destination, it's the journey." – Kobe Bryant

"The best legacies are built around service"

The actor James Dean once said, "Dream as if you'll live forever. Live as if you'll die today." No matter what the time or the hour, there is an expiration date on the lives of every single one of us.

On January 26, 2020, the world received news on the passing of a legendary, iconic American basketball player. It was as if time stopped when people heard about the tragedy of Kobe Bryant, his daughter Gianna, and the lives of seven others who were traveling with them on the helicopter that went down.

This chapter is probably one of the more difficult chapters I have written for this book. I have reverence and deep sympathy for those lives lost on that day and for their families. Throughout our lives, most of us are acutely aware that eventually there will be an end, whatever that may be to every individual.

Many of you have heard it quoted and taught that the day we leave this world behind is greater than the day that we enter it. I can see how this kind of wisdom carries a weight with it. Time and time again, we have observed the mystery and the beauty of a baby being born. We have also had to grieve the lives that have left our world and touched our hearts.

I remember exactly where I was when I received the news about Kobe Bryant. It felt as if time had completely stopped. I was in complete disbelief. I couldn't believe the news, and almost instantly after the shock had subsided and the reality sunk in, my eyes filled with tears. Even now as I articulate the moment of grief and disbelief, the emotions feel as if they are resurging. The Latin poet Vergil wrote, "No day shall erase you from the memory of time." While these words are the writings engraved on the wall of the 9/11 memorial museum, they still hold a refining influence in the hearts of all who are grieved by the loss of an extraordinary life.

Many of us grew up watching Kobe Bryant play basketball. I shared briefly in an earlier chapter that sport had a profound impact over my life. That remains true today. As I reflect on Kobe Bryant's passing, I get visual flashbacks of the times as a child where my driveway was the NBA court, and, in my mind, I was Kobe. His life emulated greatness, and to every person who looked up to him as an influential man and methodical basketball player, he was magical. His legacy will forever live on.

A TRIBUTE TO THE MAMBA MENTALITY

Kobe's accomplishments as a basketball player set him apart throughout his career on the court. Bryant's legacy, however, goes far beyond his skill and his love for basketball. He cared deeply for his family and the people he loved, and the imprint he left on the hearts of people far surpasses his celebrated career.

This is just one of the reasons that Kobe's legacy is one of greatness. He was superior both on and off the court because his mindset was unique. His actions and the way that he carried himself in the sport and in life were methodical. I believe that the way that he analyzed life was a fundamental quality that separated him from the rest of us throughout his career.

Kobe was known for the mamba mentality. When I dove in to study his life and his legacy, I discovered a quote which sums it up beautifully:

> *"You have to dance beautifully in the box that you're comfortable dancing in. My box was to be extremely ambitious within the sport of basketball. Your box is different than mine. Everybody has their own. It's your job to try to perfect it and make it as beautiful of a canvas as you can make it. And if you have done that, then you have lived a successful life. You have lived with Mamba Mentality."*

Kobe spent a lot of his time cultivating the player we all know and love. He diligently worked to prepare for victory over his opponents, studying them and putting in hours of practice when nobody was watching. He lived on a premise we discuss often as it pertains to success. It has been said several different ways, but the saying goes: *"You will be rewarded in public for what you practice in private."* As Bryant said, *"You have to work in the dark to shine in the light."*

As I've mentioned before, success does not fall into one category. Success is cultivated by determination, passion, tenacity, drive, and a lot of discipline. It is a way of not only living your life, but, once again, viewing your life.

Kobe's mamba mentality is a prime example of the mindset needed to live your life that carries a legendary legacy. In the development of this book, I did not stick to my study of people who were only successful in one avenue, particularly business. I studied greatness from all walks of life and all industries. If you wish to be great, you must study greatness.

We live in a time where our society has an infatuation with being seen and being noticed. If you don't believe me, get on TikTok. People are desperate to be seen, known, heard, and validated. I decided to write this chapter because I believe that Kobe's life epitomizes success, to a degree that we long to experience in our lives. You picked up a book to learn about success, and some people have lived a life that teaches us lessons that far outweigh the scope of lessons that are taught in any e-book or masterclass. Kobe Bryant was one of these people.

The mamba mentality teaches us the value of hard work, dedication, going the extra mile, and complete, pure obsession. The mentality of "victory or die" is the exact mentality you need to become dominant in whatever profession you're a part of. If you're gunning to be GREAT and get into the top 1% of your field, you MUST operate like Kobe operated. Kobe was willing to do whatever it took to be victorious. Sometimes, this looked a lot like encouraging his teammates and serving in any way that he could. Whether it was making sure his team was hydrated between plays, getting them water, cheering them on, or holding them accountable for their contribution as players on a team, he did so with a leadership attitude. He not only won games in basketball, but he also won in the hearts and lives of the people he encountered. That is what it takes to have a legacy. This is what it means to be successful.

LETTING LEGACY DRIVE PURSUIT

We all know that hard work and honesty alone will not bring you riches. Blessings don't come from better bank accounts. Money can solve a lot of problems, but it is not the substance of joy.

On our journey through life, we must constantly stop to see how we can be in service to others. This is where the depth of fulfillment comes. Building your life is synonymous with building your legacy. There are counterparts and stories that shape us. Benjamin Franklin once said,

"If you would not be forgotten as soon as you are dead,
either write something worth reading, or do something worth writing."

Those who have left us have given us legacies that teach us valuable lessons about the meaning we can attach to success. We don't work for money; we work for enjoyment. We provide services for money. I believe we need to examine every situation, how we can be of service to others and how we can serve our chosen industry.

As Kobe Bryant would have put it, how can you be the best in your box? Success ultimately comes down to the value you provide in the lives of others, and in the marketplace. Providing value requires that you get laser-focused and become the best that you can be. That you may give more of yourself out of passion and commitment to leaving a place better than it was before you entered.

To leave a mark, you must surrender to the trials and due diligence that mold you so that your life leaves an imprint in this world. Not every day is going to be a great day, and you will have setbacks and letdowns. But you're a champion, made in the image of God to live a life that glorifies a divine nature. Kobe Bryant's legacy left us with much to think about. His mentality leads us to reflect on a desire for greatness that for far too many becomes an empty search. As he put it:

"A lot of people say they want to be great,
but they're not willing to make the sacrifices necessary to achieve greatness."

We learn from his legacy to ask the questions that require us to make sure we are giving our all, that we put our best foot forward in service to others. Life is fleeting, and far too fragile to take for granted.

GO OUT AND BE GREAT

Words really can't paint the picture of a life lived with passion, whose legacy inspires people globally, a life like Kobe Bryant's. He taught us the value of a good attitude. He showed us the dedication and the commitment it takes to be a winner. He left us with the ultimate meaning of the mamba mentality. His success did not happen overnight, as success rarely does. It is always about the process.

For the people you see on Instagram and television, life hasn't always been simple and abundant. Success and greatness take time and sacrifice. We must remember, like Kobe Bryant did, to keep our heads up, stay in the game, and maintain an attitude of gratitude. It's hard to lose sight of your vision, to get the victory, when you appreciate every moment.

We must learn to make the necessary sacrifices to achieve greatness. We must place our dreams as the top priority and continue to work toward their realization daily. Kobe Bryant was there for his kids and his wife, but he did whatever he had to do to put in the work for success. It came as no surprise to me that Kobe was a family man, prioritizing his loved ones and the time he did get to spend with them. His family and his love for basketball came with a cost, which to my understanding was that he lost out on those extra hours of sleep. He was willing to forfeit his slumber for the attainment of success. For him success was rich relationships and passionate plays.

What does greatness mean to you? I believe that greatness can be a life well-lived, and we have many examples of that. When we look at the life of Kobe Bryant, we can confidently look toward greatness, with no obscurity about whether it's possible. When we look at Kobe Bryant, we know that **"It has Already been Done!"**

ALIVE

When we get caught up in the commotion, we can miss opportunities to become immersed in the seasons that shape much of our lives.

I have discovered that if you study how a person spends their time, you can accurately predict how they will spend most of their life. One of the greater tragedies in life is that there are many people who are physically present, but who are not alive in the most vibrant sense of the word. There is a difference between having life and being alive.

Here, I want to explore what it truly means to be alive. As I've mentioned, you and I excel further and faster when we learn to live beyond our five senses. If you cultivate these skills, the return on that investment will be resilience. Over time, your strengths will drastically change your ability to perform at the level of learning that we know as unconscious competence or mastery.

Beyond a physical pulse, have you ever stopped to consider how alive you truly are?

I want you to break free of the moronic influences of today's society. The systems within our society have capitalized on unwitting tendencies people have to attach themselves to unique identities. You and I, like every human on this planet, have been categorized. Unfortunately, many of these categories have worked against us. I am not a psychiatrist, and I am not discrediting the incredible contributions certain professionals have made toward mental health. But we can do so much better. Our society is suffering amid an epidemic of misguided, misdiagnosed, uninspired, and uninformed people, subdivided into categories created by systems that were never intended to give us the freedom of choice.

We have lost touch with our fundamental truth as creatures made in the image of God. We have settled for false identities that validate our rationalization for remaining completely unchanged. An entire generation of children is desperately trying to fit into a world that works really hard to control who they are and what they think about. By nature, this world and its systems will dish out relentless efforts to suppress people's desire to grow. They don't want you to change, to create shifts or meaningful changes, to be revolutionary, to be unwilling to give up your purpose. While there are billion-dollar corporations that pump an exorbitant amount of tax dollars into creating an illusion of good intentions, your mind, will, and emotions are at stake. James Clear, author of Atomic Habits, says, "You don't rise to the level of your goals. You fall to the level of your systems." Earlier on, I asked you if you were ready to write your story. It's a rhetorical question, because you are always telling a story. What I really meant to dig at was the beliefs that no longer serve you. What I really meant to ask you was this: are you alive?

ADAPTABLE, AWARE, AND TAKING ACTION

The night before I am to speak onstage, before I lay my head down to sleep, and then when I awaken, I run through an analysis of how I am showing up in relation to what I believe it means to be alive.

The "A" in the word "alive" is interchangeable, depending on what I am doing. It is, however, always one of these three other words: **adaptable, aware, action.**

Adaptability is the ability to shift yourself in an empowering way. If the circumstances change, we can predicate a lot of our success on our ability to adapt in a way that gives us an advantage. Learning to be adaptable is one way we build resilience. It's the art of pivoting, where the ordinary temptation would be to retreat or give up. I have also found that adaptability often accompanies a demand to level up. Whether that's learning a new skill or a method that you otherwise would have avoided, adaptability encourages growth.

When I am reflecting on things I can do to better connect within my relationships, my marriage, or my business, "A" will often represent my awareness. I have touched on awareness elsewhere in this book. I needn't stress what you should know by now — awareness is imperative to your success. There is much more that can be said on awareness, but for now, I will allow all the information I have shared on this topic to culminate to the point of revelation, which, until you realize who you are and what you want, there is nothing that I, or anyone else, can do for you.

In his book, *Your Next Five Moves: Master the Art of Business Strategy,* Patrick Bet-David shares five benefits of self-discovery and awareness. His five points are:

1. Awareness shows you that you are at the center of all your problems (and solutions).

2. You realize your problems can be fixed.

3. You crack your limiting beliefs.

4. By spotting patterns, you can end detrimental habits.

5. Your anger at others dies out once you see that no one but you controls your fate."

While success and the principles that underlie what it means to be successful are very simple; simplicity does nothing for the man or woman that will not take action.

This brings me to my favorite representation of "A" in "alive" — are you taking action?

I was listening to a speech that the actor Denzel Washington gave, when he said, "Don't confuse movement with progress, because you can run in place and not get anything done."

I wish to emphasize that you need to be intentional about how you spend your time. If painted portraits of a person's life could speak, they would tell the story of how that individual spent their time. It is entirely possible to be busy while moving backwards instead of forward. Both your choices and your efforts need to coincide with the person you have determined to be.

Your actions must align with your intended outcome. You can be incredibly ambitious while simultaneously being lazy. This, however, is a recipe for unimaginable pain. Laziness will sow seeds of negative personality traits, such as jealousy, envy, pride, and apathy. You will blame everyone else and everything else for your failures. It creates the illusion that your sh*t doesn't stink, and it can deceive you into thinking that this world owes you something. It does not, and there is no substitute for hard work.

I don't pity the person who is unwilling to humble themselves and put their head down, doing the work to create a magnificent life for themselves. In the 1994 film, The Shawshank Redemption, which detailed the double-life prison sentence of a man who was incarcerated for a crime that he didn't commit, the underlying message is that we as humans always give meaning to everything that happens on the journey we describe as our life. One of my favorite quotes from that movie is, *"You either get busy living, or you get busy dying."*

So, as you answer the question of whether you are alive, I want you to be honest with yourself. Martin Luther King Jr., said, *"The ultimate measure of a man is not where he stands in moments of comfort and convenience, but where he stands in moments of challenge and controversy."*

Are you adaptable? Have you thought long and hard about who you are and what you want?

Awareness. Finally, do your actions align with your vision, or are they merely representative of a 'woe is me' fallacy? These are some things that the A in the word alive represents to me. For some of you, it might be authenticity, for others it might be attitude. Whatever the "A" represents to you is ultimately your choice. The most important thing is that when you sit down to define what it means to be alive, you need to make sure that your actions align with what you believe.

LEARNING, LEADING, AND LAUGHING

It is only through learning that we can really prosper in our lives. Learning creates the momentum we need to move forward to the attainment of a successful life, and what that means for each of us.

We can read many books, we can conduct many studies, and we can examine many theories to come up with an antidote for living a good life. To pretend we have a definite answer to all the questions about "living a good life" would be insanity. I have read many books, and I have spent countless hours analyzing the different ways we can feel alive. In his book, The Light in the Heart, Roy T. Bennett writes, *"How much you can learn when you fail determines how far you will go in achieving your goals."*

That statement alone carries a weight that needs no added explanation. We can, however, dissect it a little further. The thing that stands out the most is that there is an action required to start a result. When I examine my life in a season where things seem to feel as though they are at a standstill, I ask myself what I am learning. This also creates an opportunity to make a choice. At any given moment in time, you can choose to learn something new. Life never requires you to feel a certain way to decide to move forward. You can be in a great place, or you can be in a place of pain. You can be in a state of peace, or you can be unsettled. Your circumstances can feel comfortable, or you can be entirely uncomfortable. You can fail, and you can succeed. The ability to choose what you will learn in these states of existence is the profound gift of being alive.

I quoted Socrates earlier: *"True wisdom comes to each of us when we realize how little we understand about life, ourselves, and the world around us."* I believe that in living a successful life is there can be no end to what you can discover. When you make learning a small priority, you make growth an impossible task.

The second thing I measure goes hand-in-hand with the first. None of us really escapes the call of leadership. It's a case of whether you are doing a good job. Like faith, leadership is something we all act out. You can lead people astray, or you can lead people toward greatness. You can lead people in the right direction, and you can also lead people off the edge of a cliff. Leadership is direction, and where you lead can be a matter of life or death – the life of a dream you have, or the death of it.

Where are you leading others? Where are you leading yourself?

Have you reflected on your journey with a good sense of humor? This is perhaps the most important question. You can take your goals seriously. In fact, you must. You can take many things seriously, but to live life requires that you do not always take yourself so seriously.

"Learning, Leading, Laughing"

What I mean by that is: in the end, none of us will make it out alive. That is the paradox of life. You learn, you lead, and the only way to make it to the finish line with some sanity is laughter. It is the ultimate medicine for the human soul. I have even heard it said that it can add years to your life. All I know is that it is the most vibrant sign of life. Life will beat all of us up from time to time. Laughter gives us the strength to keep showing up, anyway. Andrew Carnegie said it like this: *"There is little success where there is little laughter."*

INCREASING AND IMAGINATIVE

We really can't escape the revisitation of humility, especially when we are measuring how alive we truly are. In the chapter "Ethics of Success," I discussed humility. Our humility and our humanity coincide. When I discussed humility, I noted that we must sometimes decrease before we increase. Before having a panic attack in a season of decrease, ask yourself if life was trying to humble you. When I talk about increase, I am really looking at whether the odds are in my favor.

A good sign that I am living my life to the fullness of my potential is by holding myself to the standard of each of the adjectives I listed above. "Increase" is the byproduct of my ability to uphold the standards of what it means to me alive.

The second adjective that I would represent in my life is my favorite. Imaginative, directly derived from the God-given faculty of Imagination. Imagination was the author Napoleon Hill's fifth step toward wealth. Hill dedicated an entire chapter to imagination in his book *Think and Grow Rich*. Chapter six of his book perfectly illustrates the importance of this faculty, and the exact reason that I measure the depth of my life in correspondence to its use. Napoleon Hill wrote: *"MAN'S ONLY LIMITATION, within reason, LIES IN HIS DEVELOPMENT AND USE OF HIS IMAGINATION."* You can learn with ever-increasing knowledge on a subject, but knowledge has its limits. Without imagination, knowledge is useless. Imagination gives life to every single thought. Therefore, the only sure sign that you have gained any form of useful knowledge is in the practical use of your mind's ability to execute via imagination. For you and I to be truly immersed in living, we must do so from the infinite depths of our imagination.

VALUE AND VISUALIZING

If something is not adding value to your life, it is likely subtracting from it.

Value is a top-tier priority for success. When you look at value in terms of the contributions you are making, it becomes synonymous with increase, which I just discussed. When I find myself in a challenging season of life, I examine different areas of my life to see where I can contribute more.

Remember when I told you that the average person's progress is not sufficient to satisfy the need to grow? Well, when you consider your growth, or a lack thereof, one of the most underrated principles is that of value and contribution.

I can't stress enough the importance of this topic. It's really simple. You and I are adding value or wasting precious time, energy, and resources.

When you think of your life in terms of how you are contributing, you might consider a variety of areas. How are you contributing to your health? How are you contributing to your relationships? Are you constantly playing the blame game or asking what you may get from your relationships? How are you contributing to your long-term financial investments? What contributions are you making in your inner circles? Where in your life do you think you can make minor improvements every day?

Those minor improvements, compounded over time, with consistency, make up the difference between a good life and an exceptional life. Most people do as little as they can, just to get by. Success is always a long-game, and it requires constant learning, constant improvement, and constant effort. If someone taught you otherwise, they have lied to you. Brendon Burchard, bestselling author of the book High Performance Habits, said,

"If you create incredible value and information for others that can change their lives – and you always stay focused on that service – the financial success will follow."

So, when I am asking myself questions about the abundance of liveliness within my day-to-day activity, I always check to see where I could add more value or make more of a contribution.

You don't need to have a large bank account to ask these questions. It's your willingness to serve. You can contribute your time, as well as your skill sets. You can contribute by simply offering words of encouragement or helping with minor tasks around the house.

I do not limit my contribution to the amount of monthly cash flow. In fact, cash flow arguably comes from an additional meaning from the word "alive" with the letter "V" – the value you add to any area of your life. The second meaning that I'll use when I look at the "V" within the word "alive" is visualization. This is a concept I've touched on, here, and throughout my career. Are you visualizing your goals?

I don't know why daydreaming has such a negative connotation attached to it. There is a time and place to be completely lost daydreaming about one's future. Daydreaming is not the equivalent of thinking about the hamburger you want to crush during lunch. Visualization is also a very simple use of your higher faculties, specifically, your imagination.

This very simple exercise creates a profound difference in your ability to live life to its fullest meaning. One of my favorite quotes from the writer Earl Nightingale is,

> *"Visualization is the human being's vehicle to the future —*
> *good, bad or indifferent. It's strictly in our control."*

In being alive, I make sure that I am operating to the best of my ability, using my higher mental faculties. We all have to endure the hard seasons. The difference between the people who get stuck and the people who come out stronger is the use of visualization. The ability to see a clear vision of your future, and the ability to feel as though it's already happened.

ENERGY

In closing this chapter, I want to focus on one other word.

How you choose to define what it means to be alive is personal to your unique goals and experiences. Of course, modeling after someone who has achieved the results that you want is always recommended. But success is different for everybody. A life well-lived is a life of many experiences. The meaning you attach to those experiences will largely dictate the amount of joy and fullness that follows.

It's up to you to assign a representative for each of the letters in *alive*.

The word I chose carries the most amount of weight in my experience of life, and it also functions as a universal law. For me, the "E" in "alive" represents *energy*.

We see energy at work in almost every single law that governs our life, whether that is *The Law of Rhythm, The Law of Polarity, The Law of Attraction or (Vibration), The Law of Cause and Effect, etc.* Energy has a direct impact on every area of our lives. It's the reason you can walk into a room and feel empowered or exhausted. Energy can be felt in extraordinary magnitudes, or at the simple mention of your favorite song title. It can be found woven in the intricate details of tonality and communication. It literally is the cause and effect of everything in our lives.

Energy can be the very thing that creates abundance, and the very thing that enables a constant state of poverty. You are the one consistent variable in determining how the power of energy will work – for you or against you. If the people around you aren't matching the energy that uplifts you and up levels you, then you need to get with a different group of people. If the career path you've taken is not empowering you to grow, and if it's the source of low energy when you get home to your family, it's a poor investment for your future.

Whatever is not bringing you up is pulling you down or keeping you stagnant. The result is not living; it is simply existing. I don't want to come to the end of my life believing that I existed in a world with no control of how I experienced it. It's as simple as that. If you function with a low state of energy, every single result that follows will fall beneath you with a negative impact. If you function with high energy, that is positive and uplifting, your results will be positive, and your legacy will simultaneously aid in lifting the environment in which it flows, even outlasting the physical presence of your life. This, to me, is what it means to be alive.

CONCLUSION:
IN LOVING MEMORY OF BOB PROCTOR
(7/5/1934 - 2/3/2022)

*"This is an orderly universe; nothing happens by accident. The images you
plant in your marvelous mind instantly set up an attractive force which
governs your results in life.*
*You must remember, though, that this process is equally as effective
with negative images as it is with positive ones.*
*Although it is true that everything you will ever want is already here, if
not in form—in substance, it is up to you to get into harmony with it.*
*Since you do attract everything into your life by law, it would be a wise
move on your part to begin forming the habit of thinking only of what you
want, regardless of the conditions or circumstance you may presently find
yourself facing.*
To your success, Bob Proctor"

When I started the journey of writing this book, I could have never
imagined my closing remarks would be so personal and somewhat sad and
hard to write. I realize now that as I bring this book to a close that it is
actually quite the opposite of an ending. It is only the beginning. For what
it's worth, that is one of the greater ironies of life, and of success. You can
feel that you've come to the end of a road, and simultaneously, you're at the
beginning of a road.

As I write these words, there is a very real sense of infinite potential
present within the atmosphere. A very faint and very subtle tune
accompanies the feeling of possibility that moves within my atmosphere
and environment. I hear in my mind the Johnny Nash song, "I Can See
Clearly Now," as I write these words.

This is the impact of the energy that my mentor Bob Proctor carried
with him for most of his life. It is the energy that brings hope, inspires
action, and carries most of the weight in the midst of a heavy season. It's
an energy that embraces and comforts, although there is an absence of a
physical form and tangible presence. It is the energy that Bob spent his

whole life teaching, manifesting, cultivating and imparting into the lives of the many people he touched, including mine. The evidence of Bob's energy is still very much here and now. To me, that is the true effect of a legacy, the evidence of a life that was well lived.

To My Dear friend Bob,

I can't thank you enough for all that you have taught me. Your teachings and the wisdom that you poured into my life have helped me to navigate my career. I have no doubt that your instruction will continue to steer me toward the direction of possibility and infinite potential throughout my life, and the lives of generations to come. It is in this process of acceptance, harvesting the good, and forgetting the rest that I will do my utmost best to learn from and to teach from.

You left a legacy that will outlast every obstacle, and every dark and rainy day.

When I think of your life and all that you taught me, I will paraphrase the lyrics of the Johnny Nash song: "The storm clouds will clear, and there will be brighter days ahead."

Until we meet again,

Forever your student,

Alex Morton

AUTHOR'S BIO

Alex Morton is a momentum-creator, an entrepreneur, an educator and a self-made multi-millionaire. Growing up in a small Ohio town, Alex always knew he wanted more out of life. At 16, he was shoveling snow on driveways and selling cookies in the halls of his high school. At 18, as a full-time college student, he was closing residential real estate deals. At 21, he was selling vitamins and energy drinks. At 24 Alex earned his first $1 million. Today, at 33, he teaches people how to create a life of massive abundance, purpose, and fulfillment, and has spoken in over 70 countries around the world.

After realizing more than $2 billion in sales and helping over a thousand individuals earn six- and seven-figure incomes, Alex wants to teach others the sacred information that helped him build what many would call a dream life. Alex is a master at helping people take massive action toward their goals, conditioning their minds for ongoing success. "If you tell me what you want in life," Alex says, "I can show you how to get it."

Alex owes much of his success to how his parents helped train him for success in life, to his phenomenal mentor, the legendary Bob Proctor and to his incredible wife, Jane.

If you're looking for cutting-edge strategies and philosophies to help you create the business and life of your dreams, Alex is your guy.